791.43 E47j                                    FV
ELLIS
  A JOURNEY INTO DARKNESS
                    19.00

A JOURNEY INTO DARKNESS:
The Art of James Whale's
Horror Films

*This is a volume in the Arno Press Collection*

# DISSERTATIONS ON FILM 1980

*Advisory Editor*
Garth S. Jowett

*See last pages of this volume*
*for a complete list of titles*

# A JOURNEY INTO DARKNESS:
## The Art of James Whale's
## Horror Films

Reed Ellis

## ARNO PRESS

A New York Times Company
New York • 1980

Editorial Supervision: Steve Bedney

First publication in book form 1980 by Arno Press Inc.

Copyright © 1980 by Reed Ellis

Reproduced by permission of Reed Ellis

DISSERTATIONS ON FILM 1980
ISBN for complete set: 0-405-12900-9
See last pages of this volume for titles.

Manufactured in the United States of America

**Library of Congress Cataloging in Publication Data**
Ellis, Reed.
  A journey into darkness.

  (Dissertations on film 1980)
  Originally presented as the author's thesis,
University of Florida, 1979.
  Bibliography:  p.
  1.  Whale, James.  2.  Horror films--History and
criticism.  I.  Title.  II.  Series.
PN1998.A3W4774  1980    791.43'0233'0924   79-6673
ISBN 0-405-12908-4

A JOURNEY INTO DARKNESS:  THE ART OF
JAMES WHALE'S HORROR FILMS


BY


REED ELLIS


A DISSERTATION PRESENTED TO THE GRADUATE COUNCIL
OF THE UNIVERSITY OF FLORIDA IN
PARTIAL FULFILLMENT OF THE REQUIREMENTS
FOR THE DEGREE OF  DOCTOR OF PHILOSOPHY

UNIVERSITY OF FLORIDA

1979

Dedicated to
the two ladies in my life:

my Mother,
who has always supported me, financially and
emotionally, in any endeavor that I chose;

and Leslie,
who shares my happiness, tolerates my moods, picks me
up when I am down, and, most importantly, loves me

## ACKNOWLEDGMENTS

I should like to thank the following persons who have assisted me in my graduate career:

Dr. Ben Pickard, for guiding this dissertation with a firm, yet benevolent, hand;

Dr. Harry Paul, for keeping faith in me over a fifteen year period;

Dr. Alistair Duckworth, for giving me confidence in myself;

Mr. Jim Flavin and his staff, for permitting me access to the audio-visual equipment without which this study would have been, quite literally, impossible;

Mr. Dan Kennedy and his staff, for obtaining needed material in a prompt and unfailingly courteous manner;

Ms. Helen Martin and Ms. Mary Crume, for providing the best possible job environment;

and, most of all, Dr. William C. Childers, for being a close personal friend. Thanks, Bill.

# TABLE OF CONTENTS

# CHAPTER I
## INTRODUCTION

> Everything must have a beginning,
> to speak in Sanchean phrase.
>
> Mary Shelley, Frankenstein
> (Preface to 1831 edition)

> We love the thing that shocks us
> and sends chills down our spine.
>
> Carl Laemmle

> The horror film has something for
> everybody.
>
> John Simon

> I am a mere goosepimpler.
>
> James Whale

During the past ten years, the proliferation of books on film has been astounding. These works deal with a wide variety of subjects and with such diverse personalities as D. W. Griffith, Sergei Eisenstein, the Marx Brothers, John Ford, Woody Allen, and Clint Eastwood. Many of these publications focus on the work of individual directors. Yet, in all this outpouring of material, there is no book-length study of the British-born director, James Whale, although he directed some of the most interesting films of the 1930's. Indeed, several film historians do not even mention Whale's name.[1] In this study,

---

[1]Works on film history which do not give Whale even a passing glance are the following: Thomas Bohn and Richard L. Stromgren, Lights and Shadows: A History of Motion Pictures (Port Washington, N. Y.: Alfred Publishing Co., 1975); A. R. Fulton, Motion Pictures: The Development of an Art from Silent Films to the Age of TV (Norman, Okla.: University of Oklahoma Press, 1957); Lewis

1

I shall contend that Whale is an important director in the history of American film, one whose works make him worthy of consideration as a major artist.

### The Auteur Theory and James Whale

In evaluating Whale, I do not intend to subscribe to any prescribed critical formula or theory. However, since anyone who writes about an individual director is influenced to some extent by the so-called "_auteur_ theory," a brief discussion of this concept is in order.

The beginning of the "theory" dates from the mid-1950's in France. A group of young film critics who were later to become filmmakers (among them were François Truffaut, Jean-Luc Godard, and Claude Chabrol) challenged the French film "establishment." The beginning of this challenge was Truffaut's article, "A Certain Tendency of the French Cinema."[2] Truffaut--reacting against the literary bias of French film as represented by directors like Jean Dellanoy, Claude Autant-Lara, and René Clément--was outraged

---

Jacobs, _The Rise of the American Film: A Critical History_ (New York: Harcourt, Brace, and Co., 1939; reprint edition, New York: Teachers College Press, 1969); Lawrence Kardish, _Reel Plastic Magic: A History of Films and Filmmaking in America_ (Boston: Little, Brown, and Co., 1972); Arthur Knight, _The Liveliest Art: A Panoramic History of the Movies_, revised edition (New York: Macmillan Publishing Co., 1978); Kenneth W. Leish, _Cinema_ (New York: Newsweek Books, 1974); Paul Rotha, _The Film Til Now_, revised edition (London: Hamlyn Publishing Group, 1967).

[2]François Truffaut, "A Certain Tendency of the French Cinema," in _Movies and Methods: An Anthology_, ed. Bill Nichols (Berkeley and Los Angeles: University of California Press, 1976), pp. 224-238. In turn, Truffaut's ideas may be traced to Alexandre Astruc's article, "La Camera-stylo," first published in 1948. In brief, Astruc emphasized the visual component of film and argued that the director is analogous to the author of a novel. See Alexandre

by the idea that the scriptwriter, not the director, was considered the auteur of a movie. He was especially incensed by the position of France's two leading scriptwriters, Jean Aurenche and Pierre Bost, who specialized in literary adaptations: "I consider an adaptation of value only when written by a man of the cinema. Aurenche and Bost are essentially literary men and I reproach them for being contemptuous of the cinema by underestimating it "[3] (Truffaut's emphasis). In contrast to Dellanoy, Autant-Lara, Clement, Aurenche, and Bost, Truffaut favored directors such as Jean Renoir, Robert Bresson, and Max Ophuls. These men had a strong visual sense which they employed in their films and, in Truffaut's mind, they were the true auteurs of film. From Truffaut's essay, the politique des auteurs was born.

It is obvious that Truffaut's aim was a polemical one: he wanted to assert the preeminence of the director and break the literary prejudice of the French film. However, when the politique des auteurs was exported to America, excesses set in. Andrew Sarris, in his "Notes on the Auteur Theory in 1962," made the most influential American statement of the position.[4] But,

---

Astruc, "La Camera-stylo," in The New Wave, ed. Peter Graham (New York: Doubleday, 1968), pp. 17-24.

[3]Truffaut, p. 229.

[4]Andrew Sarris, "Notes on the Auteur Theory in 1962," in Film Theory and Criticism: Introductory Readings, eds. Gerald Mast and Marshall Cohen (New York: Oxford University Press, 1974), pp. 500-515.

Sarris proved to be a better writer of English than a translator
of French when he stated, "I will abbreviate la politique des
auteurs as the auteur theory to avoid confusion."[5]  He could hardly
have created more confusion, for the auteur theory is not a "theory"
at all, but a methodological tool for analysis, a way of "getting
at" and giving unity to a group of films.  At most, it may be
considered a prologomenon to a theory.  Six years later, Sarris
himself admitted that the "theory" was "not so much a theory as an
attitude,"[6] but by then the damage was done.  Sarris and his fol-
lowers established rankings and categories of directors.  In this
parlor game, for example, D. W. Griffith, Josef von Sternberg, and
Alfred Hitchcock became "Pantheon Directors," and Budd Boetticher,
Arthur Penn, and Gerd Oswald (!) were placed in the "Expressive
Esoterica" category, while such major figures as John Huston, Elia
Kazan, and Billy Wilder were consigned to the rank of "Less Than
Meets the Eye."[7]  At their most unreasonable, the auteurists
claimed that any film by, say, Alfred Hitchcock was superior to
any film by, for example, John Huston (The Maltese Falcon,
Treasure of the Sierra Madre, The African Queen), a director dis-
missed by Sarris as "virtually a forgotten man with a few actor's

---

[5]Ibid., p. 503.

[6]Andrew Sarris, The American Cinema:  Directors and Directions
1929-1968 (New York:  E. P. Dutton, 1968), p. 30.

[7]See Sarris, The American Cinema, for a complete listing of
his eleven categories.

classics behind him, surviving as the ruins of a once promising career."[8]

As early as 1957, the French film critic, André Bazin--a friend and mentor of Truffaut, Godard, and Chabrol--warned against this excessive approach. Bazin wanted "to give him [the auteur] back the preposition without which the noun auteur remains but a halting concept. 'Auteur,' yes, but of what?"[9] (Bazin's emphasis).

Although it is easy--and justifiable--to criticize the ludicrous excesses of the auteur theory, its use as an analytical tool was--and is--valid and valuable for several reasons. First, it forced critics to look at a film closely. It cleared away the bias that certain forms or genres were not worth taking seriously and re-emphasized the fact that film is primarily a visual medium.

Second, it established the director as the primary creative force behind a film. Notice that I say primary, not only. Film is undeniably a collaborative art, but this does not deny the presence of one major, shaping spirit. Hence, when I speak of James Whale's Frankenstein, I do not intend to denigrate the acting of Boris Karloff, the make-up of Jack Pierce, or the camerawork of Arthur Edeson, but to emphasize that Whale is the single most important figure in the creation of the film. I believe that this

---

[8]Sarris, "Notes on the Auteur Theory," p. 505.

[9]André Bazin, "La Politique des Auteurs," in The New Wave, p. 155.

is true even during the "studio years" of the 1930's.  As

Raymond Durgnat states,

> When all the sad truths about Hollywood have been
> allowed, it is doubtful if it cramps its best direc-
> tors' style as much as the Victorian climate of
> opinion constrained our Victorian novelists.  Indeed,
> if we allow the least literary status to, say, Robert
> Louis Stevenson, it becomes very perverse indeed to
> rule out even the "middling" films of Hitchcock,
> Hawks, Ray, and so on.[10]

Third, the auteur theory allows one to assume that, given the

fact a director may impose his own personal style upon his films,

one may learn more about a particular director's work by consid-

ering each of his films in relation to the others.  However, one

must watch one's step carefully at this juncture.  The mere fact

that a particular director possesses an individual style does not,

in and of itself, make that director's work artistic.  But if that

style is used with genius, as I believe Whale's is, then the film

becomes a work of art, and the director an artist.

Theoretically, then, the proper way to study James Whale

would be to see all his films.  Practically, the unique logistics

of film research make this impossible.  Whale made some twenty

films in a ten-year period.  Of this number, approximately ten are

available for renting (films may be bought or rented; unlike books,

they are seldom loaned).

---

[10]Raymond Durgnat, Films and Feelings (Cambridge, Mass.:
The M. I. T. Press, 1971), p. 86.

Because I possessed neither unlimited resources nor endless
time, it was necessary to limit my research. I selected Whale's
four horror films--Frankenstein (1931), The Bride of Frankenstein
(1935), The Invisible Man (1933), and The Old Dark House (1932)--
because they are his best-known works, are readily available,[11] and,
as horror films, fall into an accepted genre.

I especially wanted to select films which I could see more than
once. Until the advent of analytic projectors and video-tape equipment, it was nearly impossible to do adequate research in film.
Attempting to write from summaries of movies which one has not seen
simply does not work.[12] In addition, in order to write well about
film, it is preferable to see a film several times and to have seen
the film fairly recently, for relying on memory can be exceedingly
treacherous.[13]

---

[11]Three of the films (Frankenstein, The Bride of Frankenstein,
and The Invisible Man) are easily available. However, in order to
see The Old Dark House, I had to travel to the Library of Congress
and, then, was only able to spend a total of five hours studying
the film.

[12]Of course, it is impossible to write a large volume dealing
with a great number of films without relying to some extent on summaries. Among excellent works in various fields which do use summaries are Carlos Clarens' historical study, An Illustrated History
of the Horror Film (New York: Capricorn Books, 1968); George
Huaco's sociological examination, The Sociology of Film Art (New
York: Basic Books, 1965); Siegfried Kracauer's monumental From
Caligari to Hitler: A Psychological History of the German Film
(Princeton, N. J.: Princeton University Press, 1947; paperback
reprint edition, Princeton, N. J.: Princeton University Press,
1970); and Paul Monaco's investigation in comparative history,
Cinema and Society: France and Germany During the Twenties (New
York: Elsevier Scientific Publishing Co., 1976). Although all
these books are well done, they do contain factual errors

[13]A good example of the treachery of memory is found in John
Baxter, Hollywood in the Thirties (New York: Paperback Library,

My aim is to establish James Whale as a major artist by a
close analysis of the themes and motifs used in his horror films,
and by an examination of the stylistic cinematic tools (camera
movement, camera placement, lighting, editing, etc.) he uses to
express these themes and/or motifs. In the final analysis, Whale's
vision is extremely pessimistic and his films foreshadow the
bleakness, despair, and black comedy of such modern films as
Dr. Strangelove and Night of the Living Dead.

### The Horror Film: Definition

Any extended discussion of the horror film as genre is beyond
the scope of this paper, but a few brief comments should be made.
Though no universally agreed-upon definition of the horror film
exists, there is wide-spread agreement on its popularity. Expla-
nations for its enduring success have been many and various. For
example, Lawrence Alloway believes that there has "always been a
spontaneous human taste for monsters, for the more-than or less-
than-human";[14] Thomas Aylesworth feels that the audience is
attracted to the "mysterious, tremendous, and fascinating" power of

---

1970). This is a valuable work but Baxter, in trying to deal with
many films from memory, has confused the story of Frankenstein with
that of The Bride of Frankenstein (p. 97) and has so garbled the
plot of The Old Dark House as to make it almost unrecognizable
(p. 98). An excellent recent essay on the problem of the accuracy
of film books and the dangers of memory is Bruce Kawin, "Creative
Remembering (And Other Perils of Film Study)," Film Quarterly, v. 32
(Fall 1978), pp. 62-65.

[14]Lawrence Alloway, "Monster Films," in Focus on the Horror
Film, eds. Roy Huss and T. J. Ross (Englewood Cliffs, N. J.:
Prentice-Hall, 1972), p. 124.

the villain;[15] R. H. W. Dillard thinks that the central concern of
the horror film is to enable man to accept sin and death;[16] Drake
Douglas attributes the hold of horror movies on modern audiences to
man's "hereditary fear of the dark";[17] Walter Evans declares that
the key to the horror film's appeal is "the theme of horrible and
mysterious psychological and physical change";[18] Frank McConnell
states that the core of the genre's meaning lies in the need to
"translate and revalue the inherited burden of European culture";[19]
John Thomas asserts that through the destruction of monsters, "we
are purged of our fear of the nonhuman";[20] and Robin Wood believes
that horror films are successful because they represent "our
collective nightmares."[21]

---

[15]Thomas G. Aylesworth, Monsters From the Movies (Philadelphia:
J. B. Lippincott, 1972), pp. 16-17.

[16]R. H. W. Dillard, "Even a Man Who Is Pure at Heart: Poetry
and Danger in the Horror Film," in Man and the Movies, ed. W. R.
Robinson (Baltimore: Pelican Books, 1969), pp. 64-66.

[17]Drake Douglas, Horror! (New York: Collier Books, 1966),
p. 11.

[18]Walter Evans, "Monster Movies: A Sexual Theory," Journal of
Popular Film, v. 2 (Fall 1973), p. 354.

[19]Frank McConnell, "Rough Beasts Slouching," in Focus on the
Horror Film, p. 27.

[20]John Thomas, "Gobble, Gobble . . . One of Us!" in Focus on
the Horror Film, p. 135.

[21]Robin Wood, "Return of the Repressed," Film Comment, v. 14
(July-August 1978), p. 26.

A discussion of the horror film inevitably raises the following question: what is film genre?[22] Stuart Kaminsky defines it as a "body, group, or category of similar works; this similarity being defined as the sharing of a sufficient number of motifs so that we can identify works which properly fall within a particular kind or style of film."[23] For Stanley Solomon, "a genre film is one in which the narrative pattern, or crucial aspects of that pattern, are visually recognizable as having been used similarly in other films."[24] For my part, I am quite willing to follow Harry Geduld and Ronald Gottesman's simple description of film genre as a "category, kind or form of film distinguished by subject matter, theme, or techniques,"[25] with the stipulation that room be made in this definition

---

[22]While there have been numerous works published (both serious and trivial) on particular film genres, there has been very little written on film genre per se. The only two books devoted entirely to an overall study of film genre are Stuart Kaminsky, American Film Genres: Approaches to a Critical Theory of Popular Film (New York: Dell Publishing Co., 1977), and Stanley Solomon, Beyond Formula: American Film Genres (New York: Harcourt Brace Jovanovich, 1976). Barry K. Grant has edited a number of useful essays on film genre in Film Genre: Theory and Criticism (Metuchen, N. J.: Scarecrow Press, 1977), and Leo Braudy has an excellent chapter in his The World in a Frame: What We See in Films (New York: Anchor Press, 1977), pp. 104-181. Another very fine chapter may be found in Andrew Tudor, Image and Influence: Studies in the Sociology of Film (London: George Allen and Unwin, 1974), pp. 180-220.

[23]Kaminsky, p. 20.

[24]Solomon, p. 3.

[25]Harry M. Geduld and Ronald Gottesman, An Illustrated Glossary of Film Terms (New York: Holt, Rinehart, and Winston, 1973), p. 73.

for the emotional effect of a film upon its audience. As William
K. Everson notes, the "strong point" of the horror film is not plot,
but "audience emotion."[26]

However, the problem of just what "category, kind or form of
film" the horror film is remains. Neither Kaminsky nor Solomon gives
a real working definition of the horror film. They both devote long
chapters to the genre and attempt to isolate the themes, motifs,
icons, narrative patterns, and mythic structures of horror movies.[27]
While a listing of these elements is indispensable to studies such
as Kaminsky's and Solomon's, the underlying problem is that it is
impossible to precisely delineate the lines which separate a horror
film, a science fiction film, or a fantasy film. Is King Kong (1933)
in the horror or fantasy category? 2001: A Space Odyssey (1968) is
obviously a science fiction film, but what about Invasion of the
Body Snatchers (1956) or The Thing (1951)? This overlap of genres
is inevitable; not every film can be (or should be) strictly cate-
gorized. The best answer may be Michel Laclos' solution: group all
such films under the broad classification of the fantastic (le
Fantastique) and then one may, as Laclos does, discuss Frankenstein,
the Topper series, The Wizard of Oz (1939), It's A Wonderful Life
(1947) and Metropolis (1926) under one heading.[28]

---

[26]William K. Everson, American Silent Film (New York: Oxford
University Press, 1978), p. 219.

[27]See Kaminsky, pp. 130-154, and Solomon, pp. 111-156.

[28]Michel Laclos, Le Fantastique au Cinéma (Paris: Pauvert,
1958), pp. iii-xxxv.

For the limited purposes of this dissertation (and with no
pretense of offering a definitive definition), a horror film will
be understood to be a film whose overt aim is to terrify or
frighten, whether the events in the film are seen as impossible
fantasies (Frankenstein, The Bride of Frankenstein, The Invisible
Man) or as heightened extensions of ordinary behavior (The Old Dark
House). This emphasis on emotional effect seems to me as justi-
fiable a way of defining the horror film as a listing of icons and
motifs. As D. L. White has pointed out, if Psycho were "analyzed
not in terms of impact, but in terms of icons and plot patterns,"
it "would seem to be more a crime film than a work of horror,"[29]
yet surely no one would seriously dispute Psycho's right to be
called a horror film. By the same token, Frankenstein, The Bride of
Frankenstein, and The Invisible Man, if defined solely by their
icons and themes, could well be considered science fiction films.[30]

---

[29]D. L. White, "The Poetics of Horror: More Than Meets the
Eye," in Film Genre: Theory and Criticism, p. 127.

[30]Indeed, several critics have taken this approach. Margaret
Tarratt, "Monsters From the Id," in Film Genre: Theory and Criticism,
pp. 172-174, discusses Frankenstein and The Bride of Frankenstein as
science fiction films; John Baxter, Science Fiction in the Cinema
(New York: Paperback Library, 1970), pp. 50-51, and Douglas
Menville and R. Reginald, Things To Come: An Illustrated History
of the Science Fiction Film (New York: New York Times Book Co.,
1977), pp. 46-47, see The Invisible Man as a science fiction film;
and Jeff Rovin, From Jules Verne to Star Trek: The Best of Science
Fiction Movies and Television (New York: Drake Publishers, 1977),
pp. 10-11, 51-52, 64, believes all three films are science fiction.

In addition, Carlos Clarens observes that to study Roman Polanski's
Rosemary's Baby "as genre is quite a different matter from studying
this particular work in and of itself, or as a part of Polanski's
filmography, or even as a part of contemporary filmmaking."[31]  These
same words might easily be applied to any of Whale's horror films.
Obviously, Clarens' various ways of looking at a film overlap, but
the main thrust of this dissertation is not toward a discussion of
Whale's films as genre (although, of course, reference to the four
films as horror films will be made frequently), but as expressions
of the unique artistry of his filmography.

### The Horror Film:  History

The horror film occupies a paradoxical position in film history.
Unlike genres such as the gangster film or the musical comedy, the
horror film is not an indigenous American form, though it may
have attained its highest artistic status at Universal Studios
in the 1930's.[32]  In fact, Universal seems to have invented

---

[31]Carlos Clarens, "Horror Films," in Rediscovering the American
Cinema, ed. Douglas J. Lemza (New York:  Pioneer Press, 1977), p. 42.

[32]A definitive history of Universal Studios has yet to be
written.  I. G. Edmonds' Big U:  Universal in the Silent Days (New
York:  A. S. Barnes, 1977), is poorly written, badly organized, and
abysmally edited.  It is almost useless, although it does offer some
insight into Carl Laemmle, the founder of Universal.  Michael Fitzgerald's Universal Pictures:  A Panoramic History in Words, Pictures,
and Filmographies (New Rochelle, N. Y.:  Arlington House, 1977), is
a huge book (almost 800 pages) and has an indispensable filmography.
However, Fitzgerald's text is very slim and wholly inadequate.
Despite my previous critical comments, John Baxter's chapter on
Universal, pp. 95-118, in his Hollywood in the Thirties is a
valuable aid.  Stephen Pendo's essay, "Universal's Golden Age of
Horror:  1931-1941," Films in Review, v. 26 (March 1975), pp. 155-
161, contains a handy list of key films, but no interpretive

14

the term, "horror" film. Frankenstein was not called a horror film
in any contemporary reviews, but, four years later, The Bride of
Frankenstein was.[33]  Wherever the specific term may have originated,
the roots of horror movies are found in Europe.

The father of imagination in cinema is the Frenchman, Georges
Méliès. As Carlos Clarens aptly states, "ghoulies, ghosties, and
all things that go bump on the screen are forever in his debt."[34]

---

material. The major Universal horror films of the 1930's and
1940's are perceptively discussed by William K. Everson, "A Family
Tree of Monsters," Film Culture, v. 1 (January 1955), pp. 24-30.

[33]This surely refutes Ivan Butler's statement in Horror in the
Cinema, 2nd revised edition (New York: A. S. Barnes, 1970), p. 11,
that the term, horror film, came into general use only in the early
1950's. The contemporary reviews in which The Bride of Frankenstein
is called a horror film are Frank S. Nugent, "The Bride of Frankenstein," New York Times, 11 May 1935, p. 21, and "The Bride of
Frankenstein," Time, v. 25 (29 April 1935), p. 52.

[34]Carlos Clarens, An Illustrated History, p. 8. Clarens' book
is easily the best history of horror films available. It is comprehensive, accurate, and well-written. Its only defect is that it is
now ten years out of date. Ivan Butler's Horror in the Cinema is
also a good work and contains a useful chronology as an appendix.
William K. Everson's Classics of the Horror Film (Secaucus, N. J.:
Citadel Press, 1974), while not strictly a history, is an excellent
volume, particularly on films of the 1930's and 1940's. However,
Everson has little interest in modern horror films. A very good
short introduction to the history of the genre is Robert F. Moss,
Karloff and Company: The Horror Film (New York: Pyramid Publi-
cations, 1973). An interesting discussion of the modern horror
film (1960 to the present) may be found in Charles Derry, Dark
Dreams: A Psychological History of the Modern Horror Film (New
York: A. S. Barnes, 1977). Other histories of lesser merit
include Thomas G. Aylesworth, Monsters From the Movies; Edward
Edelson, Great Monsters of the Movies (Garden City, N. Y.:
Doubleday, 1973); Alan G. Frank, Horror Movies (London: Octopus
Books, 1974); Denis Gifford, A Pictorial History of Horror Movies
(London: Hamlyn Publishing Group, 1973); Tom Hutchinson, Horror
and Fantasy in the Movies (New York: Crescent Books, 1974); Frank
Manchel, Terrors of the Screen (Englewood Cliffs, N. J.: Prentice-
Hall, 1970); and Ed Naha, Horrors: From Screen to Scream (New York:
Avon Books, 1975).

Méliès pioneered in the use of double exposure, multiple exposure,
fast motion, slow motion, stop motion, the fade, and the dissolve.
In such films as A Trip to the Moon (1902) and The Conquest of the
Pole (1912), Méliès laid the groundwork for science fiction, horror,
and fantasy films.

From France, the family tree of horror film branches out to
Germany and the single most important influence on the horror genre,
German Expressionism.[35]  The German Expressionist movement in film
was primarily influenced by Expressionist painting and by the
theatre of Max Reinhardt.  German Expressionist painters were a
varied group who never formed a monolithic unit (some of their
better-known members were Max Pechstein, Marc Kandinsky, Oscar
Kokoschska, and Max Beckmann); they were influenced by such anti-
naturalist artists as Edvard Munch, Vincent van Gogh, and Paul

---

[35]The premier work on German films of the 1920's is Siegfried
Kracauer's famous From Caligari to Hitler.  While not a study of
Expressionism in itself, Kracauer's book is required reading for any-
one working with German films.  Part of Kracauer's thesis, that the
German film in its themes and style prefigures the rise of Hitler,
is, at least, plausible.  The idea that the films reflect the
German people's "deep psychological dispositions" (p. v) toward
tyranny and authoritarianism is, at best, questionable.  Lotte
Eisner's The Haunted Screen:  Expressionism and the Influence of Max
Reinhardt (Berkeley and Los Angeles:  University of California Press,
1973), convincingly demonstrates Reinhardt's influence.  However, it
is sloppily organized and poorly written, and also marred by such
ridiculous statements as "the German soul instinctively prefers
twilight to daylight" (p. 51).  George Huaco's chapter on German
Expressionism, pp. 25-92, in his The Sociology of Film Art, is a
solid essay.  Roger Manvell and Heinrich Fraenkel's The German
Cinema (New York:  Praeger, 1971), provides a useful summary of
Expressionism, but adds no new insights.  Of particular value among
shorter studies is Andrew Tudor's chapter in Image and Influence,
pp. 155-179.

Cézanne. Expressionism in painting was an attempt to break away
from Impressionism and to present an individual's subjective inner
vision. In depicting this inner state of mind, the Expressionists
departed from naturalistic forms and colors and tended toward por-
traying a radical deformation of the natural order. Eventually,
many of the set designers and art directors for German films would
be recruited from the ranks of Expressionist painters.[36]

The second major influence on German film Expressionism was the
master stage director, Max Reinhardt. Reinhardt's work on the stage
with group composition, lighting, and architectural form was enormously
influential on the film. Many of Germany's top cinema directors--such
as Paul Leni, F. W. Murnau, and Karl Grune--as well as the top actors--
such as Paul Wegener, Werner Krauss, Conrad Veidt, and Emil Jannings--
had all worked for Reinhardt.[37]

The beginning of German Expressionism in films is always dated
from The Cabinet of Dr. Caligari (1919), but the ending date is
vague. Andrew Tudor places the end of Expressionism in 1926 with
The Student of Prague, Faust, and Metropolis, while Lotte Eisner
extends the movement through the coming of sound in 1931 with The
Blue Angel, The Three Penny Opera, and M.[38] It may be safely stated

---

[36]For a good short background study of the Expressionist
painters, see Huaco, pp. 69-73.

[37]See Huaco, p. 87, for information on the directors, and
Eisner, p. 44, for documentation on the actors.

[38]Tudor, p. 156, and Eisner, pp. 314-323.

that Expressionism had spent its force by the mid-1920's and the trend was toward realism, although many Expressionist techniques continued to be employed in realist films.

The style of the Expressionist cinema was characterized by the use of diagonals and broken angles, the unique utilization of light and shadow, large objects (houses, doorways, etc.) which were noticeably tilted and either too large or too small in relation to human beings, the employment of abrupt, stylized acting techniques, and, most importantly for the future art of the film, the use of a mobile, moving camera to portray an individual's subjective viewpoint.

The themes of Expressionism were grouped around the idea of man's powerlessness before "destiny," i.e., the inevitability of "Fate" (F. W. Murnau's The Last Laugh, Fritz Lang's Destiny); the concept of the divided self and the duality of life (Henrik Galeen's The Student of Prague, Robert Wiene's The Cabinet of Dr. Caligari); and the power of the supernatural to influence one's life (Paul Wegener's The Golem, Murnau's Faust).

As direct influences on the Frankenstein series, three Expressionist films--Caligari, The Golem, and Metropolis--are especially important and will be discussed in more detail in Chapter II.

The American silent cinema provided little inspiration for the great Universal horror cycle of the 1930's. There were, however, a number of silent films known as "thrillers" or "shockers," such as John S. Robertson's Dr. Jekyll and Mr. Hyde (1920) with John Barrymore in the title role and, in particular, the films of Lon

Chaney. During the 1920's, Chaney created one brilliant role after another, the most important and influential being the Phantom in The Phantom of the Opera (1926). As Clarens states, "the character of the Phantom, combining the attributes of musical genius, master builder, and ruthless killer, is an early version of the sympathetic monster-villain."[39] Also, there was a series of influential "old house" thrillers, like Roland West's The Bat (1926), Alfred Santell's The Gorilla (1927), and, especially, Paul Leni's The Cat and the Canary (1927). As the most important of these films and as an influence on The Old Dark House, The Cat and the Canary will be discussed in greater detail in Chapter V.

By 1930, all was in readiness for the horror film to burst forth as an art form. "The stylistic influences from Germany . . . the long-developed commercial tradition of the 'shockers' and the line in individual grotesquerie pioneered by Chaney, all combined in the Universal melting pot."[40] All that was needed was a master chef to produce an artistic brew from this "melting pot." The time was right for James Whale.

### James Whale: An Overview

"James Whale, who directed the movie Frankenstein, died today after falling into the swimming pool of his home. He was 60 years

---

[39]Clarens, An Illustrated History, p. 50

[40]Tudor, p. 204.

old."[41] The New York Times obituary is, like many statements
about Whale's career and his films, inaccurate. He was not sixty;
he was sixty-seven. For years, his birthdate was accepted as
July 21, 1896, but he was actually born in 1889, and apparently used the false date because of vanity.[42]

At the time of his death, Whale was a forgotten man. Only
one commemorative article appeared in any journal or magazine.[43]
Even today, it is almost impossible to obtain detailed biographical
information on Whale, and what is obtainable is often incorrect.[44]

---

[41]"Obituary: James Whale," New York Times, 30 May 1957, p. 23.

[42]John Brosnan, The Horror People (New York: St. Martin's
Press, 1976), p. 67; Tom Milne, "One Man Crazy: James Whale,"
Sight and Sound, v. 43 (Summer 1973), p. 166; Don Whittemore and
Philip Alan Cecchettini, "Orientation to James Whale," in Pass-
port to Hollywood: Film Immigrants Anthology, eds. Don Whittemore
and Philip Alan Cecchettini (New York: McGraw-Hill, 1976), p. 271.

[43]Roy Edwards, "Movie Gothick: A Tribute to James Whale,"
Sight and Sound, v. 28 (Autumn 1957), pp. 95-98.

[44]Short entries on Whale may be found in the following film
reference works: Liz-Anne Bawden, ed., The Oxford Companion to
Film (New York: Oxford University Press, 1976), pp. 748-749;
Leslie Halliwell, The Filmgoer's Companion, 4th edition (New
York: Hill and Wang, 1974), p. 800; Roger Manvell, ed., The
International Encyclopedia of Film (New York: Crown Publishers,
1972), p. 502; Georges Sadoul, Dictionary of Film Makers, ed.
and trans. Peter Morris (Berkeley and Los Angeles: University
of California Press, 1972), p. 275; John M. Smith and Tim Cawkwell, eds., The World Encyclopedia of the Film (New York: World
Publishing Co., 1972), p. 292; David Thomson, A Biographical
Dictionary of Film (New York: William Morrow, 1976), pp. 611-
612. Not one of these works is without error. Both the
International Encyclopedia and the World Encyclopedia give Whale's
birthdate as 1896, and both also identify him as a "theatrical

Whale was born in Dudley, Worcestershire, England.  His
father, William Whale, was an ironworker and secretary of the trade
union which he had helped found.  His mother, Sarah Whale, was a nurse.
Thus, Whale, who projected an image of the cultivated, urbane,
upper-class Englishman, was from a working class background, and he
always retained an interest in social behavior and the English
class system which is evidenced in his horror films, particularly
The Old Dark House.

Whale left Dudley shortly after 1910 and got a job  in
London as a cartoonist for the magazine, The Bystander.  When World
War I began, he obtained a commision as a second lieutenant with
the Seventh Worcester Infantry Regiment and was sent to France.
His war service was brief, for he was captured soon after arriving

producer."  Whale was never a producer, but a theatre director.
The usually reliable Leslie Halliwell has Whale's birthdate as
1886 (however, this is obviously a typographical error since
the 3rd edition has the correct date) and identifies Whale's 1932
film, The Impatient Maiden, as The Imprudent Maiden.  The Oxford
Companion has the correct biographical information, but curiously
defines Whale's 1938 movie, Wives Under Suspicion (a remake of his
1934 psychological drama, The Kiss Before the Mirror), as a "comedy."
Georges Sadoul calls Whale a producer and makes the same title error
as Halliwell.  David Thomson has a good short essay on Whale, but
repeats the fallacy that he was a producer.  John Brosnan, The
Horror People, pp. 67-72, gives a fairly complete summary of Whale's
life, while Don Whittemore and Philip Alan Cecchettini, "Orientation
to James Whale," pp. 271-278, summarize Whale's life and most of
his films.  William Thomaier and Robert  Fink, "James Whale," Films
in Review, v. 13 (May 1962), pp. 277-289, provide useful biographical
information and a list of all the films.  Paul Jensen, "James Whale,"
Film Comment, v. 7 (Spring 1971), pp. 52-57, has a rather cursory
discussion of some of the films.  Tom Milne, "One Man Crazy," pp. 166-
170, also discusses the films briefly.  The only work of film history
which deals with Whale in any detail is Charles Higham, The Art of the
American Film:  1900-1971 (Garden City, N. Y.: Doubleday, 1973),
pp. 157-163.

at the western front. "My platoon had been told to do a stint on
a pill-box at midnight, and we had gone straight into a well-laid
trap. It all happened so suddenly I was stupefied and found it
impossible to believe myself cut off from everything British and in
the hands of the Hun."[45]

For the remainder of the war, Whale was incarcerated in a POW
camp near Hanover. During this period he began his acting career
by performing in plays put on by the camp inmates. After the war,
Whale joined the Birmingham Repertory Theatre and, in addition to
acting, did odd jobs such as designing sets for productions of The
Cherry Orchard and The Seagull.

In March, 1925, Whale acted for the first time on the London
stage in a production of A Comedy of Good and Evil at the Ambassador
Theatre. He got his big break when an unknown playwright named
R. C. Sherriff approached him about directing Sherriff's anti-war
play, Journey's End. In his autobiography, Sherriff recalls his
first meeting with Whale. "He [Whale] scarcely looked at me; he
kept his eyes on the mirror . . . and talked to my reflection in
the glass. . . . He didn't seem very enthusiastic about Journey's
End."[46] At this point in his life, Whale was, according to Sherriff,

---

[45]Thomaier and Fink, p. 285.

[46]R. C. Sherriff, No Leading Lady: An Autobiography (London:
Victor Gollancz, 1968), p. 47.

"a man of all work in the theatre. He played small parts, designed and painted scenery, and occasionally got a job as stage manager, but he had never been in charge of a play in a West End theatre. He told me later that he had never earned beyond five pounds a week for anything he had done."[47] In a sequence of events which would do credit to a Hollywood screenplay, Journey's End opened in December, 1928, and was a great success. Whale also directed the Broadway production the following year and was then contracted to direct the film version.

The film of Journey's End was released in 1930 to rave reviews and, during the next decade, Whale directed twenty films (a complete filmography may be found in Appendix A), ending his career in 1941 by walking off the set of They Dare Not Love after an argument; he never returned to commercial filmmaking, although he did make one more effort at directing. In 1949, he made a short version of William Saroyan's one-act play, Hello Out There, for the film producer, Huntington Hartford. The film was shown to a special preview audience which included Saroyan, Charlie Chaplin, John Huston, and Jean Renoir. It was well received by the audience, but Hartford was dissatisfied with the results (apparently because he felt it did not make adequate use of his wife, Marjorie Steele) and never released it.[48]

---

[47] Ibid., pp. 46-47.

[48] Brosnan, The Horror People, p. 71, and Thomaier and Fink, pp. 288-289.

Whale lived in semi-seclusion until his death. He directed a few plays (including, in 1951, The Pagan in the Parlor in England), but mostly he devoted his time to studying painting. In 1952, he toured European art museums for this purpose and, at the time of his death, was designing sets for a science fiction operetta based on the works of Ray Bradbury and Max Beerbohm.[49] He had invested his money wisely in real estate, and at his death his estate was valued at $600,000.[50]

The circumstances of Whale's death are often referred to as "mysterious." Probably because of his homosexuality, it has been rumored that some type of ritualistic, Sharon Tate-type, sexual murder took place. The truth is certainly less lurid. Whale had had a mild stroke in early 1957; he apparently had another one, fell into his pool, and simply did not have the strength to pull himself out.[51]

Whale was a shy, reticent man frequently described as "aloof."[52] Despite this aloofness, he obviously had an excellent rapport with actors and actresses since he almost always elicited good performances. He rarely gave interviews and, after he retired, there was little interest in him. Hence, the outlines of his personality are (and are likely to remain) vague.

---

[49]Thomaier and Fink, p. 289.

[50]Brosnan, The Horror People, p. 72.

[51]Ibid.

[52]Ibid.

In addition to Whale's four horror films, he made at least five
other films (The Kiss Before the Mirror, By Candlelight, One More
River, Show Boat, and The Great Garrick) which merit closer attention
than they have been given.[53]

The Kiss Before the Mirror (1933), at first glance a mere
melodrama, contains subtle psychological insights. It is heavily
influenced by the Expressionist style (Karl Freund, the famous
cameraman for The Last Laugh, was the cinematographer) and, according to Charles Higham, includes "more authentic terrors" than the
horror films.[54] The film concerns a doctor, Walter Bernsdorf (Paul
Lukas), who murders his wife, Lucie (Gloria Stuart), because of her
infidelity. The defense attorney, Paul Held (Frank Morgan), finds
many similarities between his life and his client's, including the
fact that his own wife, Maria (Nancy Carroll), is also unfaithful.
Held becomes more and more closely identified with Bernsdorf,
indicating Whale's interest in paired characters, an interest which
also infuses his horror films. Another major concern of Whale's is
shown by his emphasis on characters' external images; the Monster's
exterior appearance is also a major motif in Frankenstein and The

---

[53]It is outside the focus of this paper to do more than briefly
mention these films. Of the five, I have seen The Kiss Before the
Mirror, Show Boat, and The Great Garrick, but have had no opportunity
to study them in depth. I have not seen By Candlelight or One More
River and have relied on the judgment or others, an admittedly
dangerous procedure.

[54]Higham, The Art of the American Film, p. 159.

Bride of Frankenstein. The movie climaxes with a surrealist court-
room scene in which Held sounds a Kafka-esque "we are all guilty"
theme by arguing that, given sufficient provocation, anyone might
act as Bernsdorf acted.

William K. Everson, Whale's most perceptive critic, has called
By Candlelight (1933) one of Whale's three best films.[55] The plot
revolves around the reversal of roles between a master and his
servant, and gives Whale a chance to explore the use of artificial
roles and poses, a topic also examined in The Old Dark House.

In One More River (1934), Whale's version of John Galsworthy's
last novel, he "demonstrates his acute and accurate insight into
social life."[56] Whale is always interested in the social and
emotional lives of his characters, even when those characters are
the monsters and grotesques which populate his horror films. This
film of a woman seeking a divorce from her sadistic husband has been
called Whale's "masterpiece" by Everson.[57]

In 1936, Whale was at the peak of his career and Universal
tapped him to direct their "big picture" of the year, Show Boat.

---

[55]William K. Everson, "Rediscovery: Journey's End," Films in
Review, v. 26 (January 1975), p. 32.

[56]Whittemore and Cecchettini, p. 275.

[57]William K. Everson, "Rediscovery: One More River," Films in
Review, v. 26 (June-July 1975), p. 362.

Although Whale had no experience with musicals, the film was a huge
success, financially and artistically. The opening sequence,
showing the arrival of the show boat, is a tour de force of editing.
Whale perfectly conveys the frenzied excitement which the boat's
arrival occasions as he cuts breathlessly from the boat to shots of
people, horses, and even a sow with her piglets, all rushing to
greet the "Cotton Blossom." Whale's sense of camera movement and
editing is graphically displayed in another scene. Paul Robeson,
seated on a wharf, sings "Ol' Man River"; as Robeson sings, Whale
swings the camera in a 360° pan around him, perfectly complementing
the words of the song with shots of the Mississippi "rolling along,"
and subtly commenting on the racial situation by intercutting an
Expressionist montage of slavery. Scenes such as the two above lead
Higham to call Show Boat Whale's "most purely cinematic film."[58]

After Show Boat, it is customary to conclude that Whale's
career declined, but The Great Garrick (1937) is hardly such. The
story revolves around a visit the British actor, David Garrick (Brian
Aherne), pays to France. The members of the Comédie Française,
annoyed by Garrick's slur about French acting, contrive to trick him
by taking over an inn where Garrick is staying, and acting the parts
of the servants. Again, Whale deals with the influence of roles
and poses on human life and behavior. He explores the question,
"must emotions be real to be believable or is only the communication

---

[58]Higham, The Art of the American Film, p. 160.

real?"[59] The film ends in what Tom Milne calls a "double check-mate."[60] Garrick correctly realizes that the actors are playing roles, but falsely assumes that Germaine (Olivia de Havilland) is part of the plot while, in fact, her emotional feelings for Garrick are real. The Great Garrick deserves more careful scrutiny than it has been given in order to thoroughly analyze the reality-illusion theme which is the core of the film.

Many more questions remain about Whale's output. For example, is Remember Last Night? (1935) really a forerunner of the French "New Wave,"[61] or is it only "good minor fun"?[62] Is The Road Back (1937), Whale's rendition of Erich Maria Remarque's novel, "an unsuccessful attempt to recapture the greatness of Journey's End,"[63] or an "entirely serious [film] in its approach to the difficulties of readjustment faced by young war veterans" after World War I in Germany?[64] And why is Port of Seven Seas (1938), a film not even mentioned in two of the works I have previously cited,[65] called

---

[59]Whittemore and Cecchettini, p. 276.

[60]Milne, p. 170.

[61]Ibid., p. 168.

[62]André Sennwald, "Remember Last Night?" New York Times, 21 November 1935, p. 27.

[63]Higham, The Art of the American Film, p. 163.

[64]Milne, p. 166.

[65]Neither Higham, The Art of the American Film, nor Whittemore and Cecchettini acknowledge the film's existence.

"queerly beautiful"[66] and a film of "quiet, anecdotal charm"[67] by contemporary reviewers?

Clearly, any definitive assessment of Whale's career must await the unearthing and careful examination of his as yet largely disregarded _oeuvre_.

---

[66]B. R. Crisler, "_Port of Seven Seas_," _New York Times_, 15 July 1938, p. 13.

[67]"_Port of Seven Seas_," _Time_, v. 32 (11 July 1938), p. 42.

CHAPTER II
FRANKENSTEIN

Have you never wanted to look
beyond the clouds and the stars,
or to know what causes the trees
to bud?  And what changes darkness
into light?

Henry Frankenstein (to
Dr. Waldman)

Think of it!  The brain of a dead
man waiting to live again in a body
I made with my own hands!  With my
own hands!

Henry Frankenstein

You have created a Monster and it
will destroy you.

Dr. Waldman (to Henry
Frankenstein)

## Influences on the Frankenstein Films

Prior to James Whale's 1931 Frankenstein, there were two

silent American versions of Mary Shelley's novel--Frankenstein in

1910, produced by the Edison Corporation, and Life Without Soul

in 1915, produced by the Ocean Film Corporation.[1]  However,

neither of these films influenced Whale's version.  The chief

forerunners of Whale's Frankenstein were three German Expressionist

films--The Cabinet of Dr. Caligari (1919), The Golem (1920), and

Metropolis (1926).

------

[1] Carlos Clarens, An Illustrated History of the Horror Film
(New York:  Capricorn Books, 1968), pp. 38-39, and Donald F. Glut,
The Frankenstein Legend:  A Tribute to Mary Shelley and Boris
Karloff (Metuchen, N. J.:  Scarecrow Press, 1973), pp. 58-67.
Glut's exhaustive survey is an attempt to document every

29

The Cabinet of Dr. Caligari[2] is a legendary film, universally recognized as the beginning of the German Expressionist movement.[3] The angular, distorted sets were the work of Hermann Warm, Walter Röhrig, and Walter Reimann (they had all been Expressionist painters), the script was written by Carl Mayer and Hans Janowitz, and the direction was by Robert Wiene. According to Paul Jensen, Whale screened Caligari just before beginning Frankenstein,[4] and its influence shows primarily in the mise-en-scène (the style and decor) of the later film. For instance, the scene in Caligari in which Cesare (Conrad Veidt) enters Jane's (Lil Dagover) room intending to kill her is noticeably similar in its tone and in the contrasts of blacks and whites to the scene in Frankenstein when the Monster enters Elizabeth's room. The parallel continues when Cesare, disobeying Dr. Caligari's (Werner Krauss) orders, refuses to kill Jane, just as the Monster only frightens Elizabeth.

The individual's mad lust for power is another theme of Caligari which is reflected in Frankenstein and The Bride of

---

appearance of the Frankenstein legend in print, on the stage, and on film.

[2]Hereafter, references to The Cabinet of Dr. Caligari will be abbreviated as Caligari.

[3]For a comprehensive account of the making of Caligari, see Seigfried Kracauer, From Caligari to Hitler: A Psychological History of the German Film (Princeton, N. J.: Princeton University Press, 1947; paperback reprint edition, Princeton, N. J.: Princeton University Press, 1970), pp. 61-76.

[4]Paul Jensen, Boris Karloff and His Films (New York: A. S. Barnes, 1974), p. 28.

Frankenstein.[5] For example, Dr. Caligari closely resembles Dr.
Pretorius in Bride. As Martin Tropp notes,    there is a striking
parallel scene which points up this connection between Caligari and
Bride.[6] In Caligari, Dr. Caligari, holding a staff in his hand,
stands beside Cesare, who is sleeping upright in his coffin-like box.
In Bride, Dr. Pretorius stands next to the Monster, who is framed
in a box-like open doorway, while a spear is seen leaning on the
wall beside Pretorius. In each instance, the staff and the spear
function as symbols of domination and power.

It is dangerous, however, to press the resemblances of
Caligari and the Frankenstein films too far since, as Ivan Butler observes, Caligari is a germinal film within which the seeds
of almost all future horror films may be found.

> In Caligari may be found in rudimentary form  most of
> the basic ingredients of the horror film formulae of
> later years:  the mad scientist and the monster (both
> inherent in the Doctor)--the 'undead' and the zombie
> (the somnambulist who sleeps in a coffin-shaped box
> and automatically follows his master's commands)--the
> girl dragged around in white flowing draperies--the
> general feeling of isolation and claustrophobia.[7]

Metropolis (1926), a heady mixture of incredible architectural compositions and even more incredible political naivete,

---

[5]Hereafter, The Bride of Frankenstein will frequently be
abbreviated as Bride.

[6]Martin Tropp, Mary Shelley's Monster:  The Story of
Frankenstein (Boston:  Houghton Mifflin, 1976), p. xii.

[7]Ivan Butler, Horror in the Cinema, 2nd revised edition
(New York:  A. S. Barnes, 1970), pp. 21-22.

has been called the "last gasp of Expressionism" in Fritz Lang's work.[8] This film supposedly prompted Hitler to offer Lang the position of head of the Third Reich film division (Lang left Germany in 1933 while his wife, Thea von Harbou, stayed and worked with Goebbels).[9] The film's influence on the Frankenstein films lies in only one sequence, but that sequence is a very important one: the creation by Rotwang (Rudolf Klein-Rogge) of the "robot Maria" (Brigitte Helm).

Although the staid editing in Metropolis is in no way comparable to Whale's sophisticated techniques, the machine creation of the "false Maria," with its spinning dials, glowing coils, and, especially, its use of electricity as the life force, obviously foreshadows the creation scenes in Frankenstein and Bride. Also, the first jerky movements of Brigitte Helm (she was later considered for the part of the Monster's mate in Bride)[10] as the robot are similar to Elsa Lanchester's movements in Bride.[11]

---

[8]Clarens, An Illustrated History, p. 31. Herman Weinberg relates an amusing anecdote about Lang and Expressionism. According to Weinberg, Lotte Eisner once asked Lang to chair a symposium on Expressionism. Lang asked Weinberg, "What did she mean by a symposium on Expressionism? What's Expressionism?" Weinberg had to give Lang a quick course in Expressionism before he was able to address the symposium (Herman Weinberg, "Coffee, Brandy and Cigars," Take One, v. 6 (July 1978), p. 40).

[9]Clarens, An Illustrated History, p. 36.

[10]Denis Gifford, A Pictorial History of Horror Movies (London: Hamlyn Publishing Group, 1973), p. 111.

[11]Both William K. Everson, Classics of the Horror Film Secaucus, N. J.: Citadel Press, 1974), p. 20, and Glut, The Frankenstein Legend, pp. 82-83, state that Whale was influenced, particularly regarding the laboratory sets, by Rex Ingram's The

Unquestionably, the single most influential film on the
Frankenstein series is Paul Wegener's 1920 version of The Golem,
which was made for the huge German film conglomerate, Universum
Film A. G. (UFA).[12] The Golem (Paul Wegener) is a giant creature
made of clay who is given life by magical means. Animated when a
magical word is enclosed in a Star of David amulet and placed on
his chest, he protects the Jewish inhabitants of the Prague ghetto
from the threatened sanctions of the Christian emperor.

The most obvious resemblance between The Golem and Frankenstein
is the creation of an artificial being, with the significant difference that the Golem is created by magic, the Monster by science.
Fire, an important symbolic element in Frankenstein, is also present
in the Golem's creation, as Rabbi Loew (Albert Steinruck), the
Golem's creator, stands in the center of a circle of fire while
uttering his magical incantation. Wegener's stiff-legged walk is
similar to the Monster's first hesitant steps. However, Wegener

---

Magician (1926), based on the career of the notorious Aleister
Crowley. This film, thought for years to be lost, has recently
re-surfaced, but I have not been able to see it and cannot verify
its influence.

[12]There is general agreement among film historians that UFA
was a virtual monopoly which controlled German filmmaking during
the 1920's. However, this view has been disputed by Paul Monaco,
Cinema and Society: France and Germany During the Twenties (New
York: Elsevier Scientific Publishing Co., 1976), pp. 29-30,
and H. H. Wollenberg, Fifty Years of German Film (London: Falcon
Press, 1948; reprint ed., New York: Arno Press, 1972), p. 17.

never varies this zombie-like movement, whereas Karloff's motions become more assured as the Monster matures.

The most important similarity between the two films is the development of emotional feelings by each of the creatures. The Golem is first emotionally moved when he is given a flower (flowers are also symbolically important in Frankenstein) by one of the celebrants at the Rose Festival (this festival may be seen as a forerunner of the wedding celebration in Frankenstein). The Golem continues to develop emotionally by falling in love with Miriam (Lyda Salmonova), Rabbi Loew's daughter. Rabbi Loew, like Henry Frankenstein, loses control of his creation, who promptly sets fire to the Rabbi's home and decimates the ghetto. In a scene which clearly prefigures the Monster's sequence with Maria in Frankenstein, the Golem is finally destroyed when a little girl, the only person who shows no fear of the creature, removes the amulet from his breast while playing with him.[13]

Viewed today, The Golem is still an impressive film, holding up much better than most silent movies. Obviously, Whale borrowed many elements from The Golem, but he used a much more complex visual style to infuse Frankenstein and Bride with a richer texture of meaning.

---

[13]Two other minor parallels between The Golem and the Frankenstein films are the use of an assistant (Ernst Deutsch) for Rabbi Loew (just as Henry has Fritz in Frankenstein) and a scene in which the Golem throws Miriam's lover, Florian (Hans Sturm), off a tower, remarkably similar to the sequence in Bride where the Monster tosses Karl to his death.

## Background: Frankenstein

Universal had owned the film rights to Frankenstein since
1920,[14] but the studio had been hesitant to make the film,
considering it a poor financial risk. However, after the success
of Dracula (released in February, 1931), the Laemmles (Carl,
Senior, the founder of Universal, and Carl, Junior, production
chief) decided to proceed. The history of the making of Frankenstein
is filled with contradictions and discrepancies. Today, with almost all the principals involved deceased, it is impossible to
arrive at one "true" account. Nevertheless, the broad outlines
of the story are reasonably distinct.[15]

Robert Florey, a French director, was originally scheduled
to direct the film and actually blocked out a scenario containing
some 600 scenes.[16] A screen test, with Florey directing and

---

[14]Denis Gifford, Karloff: The Man, the Monster, the Movies
(New York: Curtis Books, 1973), p. 37. By the time Universal
decided to make the film, Peggy Webling had written a stage
version and the studio also purchased--in April, 1931--the rights
to her work, probably to avoid any possibility of a plagiarism
suit (Jensen, Boris Karloff, p. 28).

[15]The best treatment of Frankenstein's background is found
in Gifford, Karloff, pp. 37-56; Glut, The Frankenstein Legend,
pp. 90-120; and Jensen, Boris Karloff, pp. 23-44.

[16]Robert Florey, Hollywood d'Hier et d'Aujourd'hui (Paris:
Editions Prisma, 1948), p. 163. Florey relates the following
amusing interview with Laemmle, Junior: "In the course of a
single interview, while Carl Laemmle, Junior, gave his fingers
to a manicurist, his hair to a hairdresser, his thoughts to his
secretaries, and his voice to a dictaphone, I explained the
general plan of the film to him. He told me to quickly type my
story and give it to the head of the screenplay department"
(Florey, p. 164). The original French is as follows: "Au cours

Bela Lugosi as the Monster, was actually shot on the set of
Dracula. What happened next is unclear. Lugosi stated that he
did not like the script and wanted out of the picture. However,
it is equally possible that Laemmle, Junior, cancelled the project.[17] The truth seems to be a combination of these two stories.
Lugosi was unquestionably a vain man who was proud of his speaking
voice and saw himself as something of a Hungarian Rudolf Valentino.[18]

---

d'une singulière entrevue, tandis que Carl Laemmle livrait ses
doigts à la manicure, ses chevaux au coiffeur, ses pensées à ses
secretaires, et sa voix à son dictaphone, je lui expliquai le plan
général du film. Il me demanda de dactylographier rapidement mon
histoire et de la remettre au chef du département des scénarios."
The translation is mine.

[17]According to Lugosi, "I made up for the role and had tests
taken, which were OK. Then, I read the script and didn't like
it. So I asked to be withdrawn from the picture. Carl Laemmle
said he'd permit it if I'd furnish an actor to play the part. I
scouted the agencies--and came upon Boris Karloff. I recommended
him" (Jensen, Boris Karloff, p. 23). In a slightly different
version of this story, Calvin Thomas Beck states that Lugosi turned
the part down because it had no dialogue, then called Karloff and
told him the part was "nothing but might mean some money for him"
(Calvin Thomas Beck, Heroes of the Horrors (New York: Collier
Books, 1975), p. 113). Denis Gifford says that Laemmle, Junior,
cancelled the movie after seeing the tests and "Lugosi put it
about that he had rejected the role on the grounds that it had
no dialogue" (Gifford, Karloff, p. 37). John Brosnan agrees with
Gifford's account in The Horror People (New York: St. Martin's
Press, 1976), p. 30. Florey, p. 164, remarks only that Lugosi
"did not show much enthusiasm for the role and did not want to
play it." Florey's original French is as follows: ". . . ne se
montra pas très enthousiastic du rôle et ne voulut pas l'interpréter."
The translation is mine.

[18]According to David Zinman, Fifty Classic Motion Pictures
(New York: Crown Publishers, 1970), p. 179, Lugosi once proudly
boasted that he received 97 per cent of his fan mail from women.

He obviously did not like the idea that the role had no dialogue.[19]

In addition, Laemmle definitely did not like the screen test

results.[20] In short, Lugosi wanted out of the picture and Laemmle

was glad to let him go.

About the same time that Lugosi left, Florey departed also.

Again, the reasons and the sequence of events are hazy. According

to Florey,

> James Whale, the ace of Universal, demanded that Carl
> Laemmle let him film Frankenstein, which had been prom-
> ised to me. He satisfied Whale without, however, informing
> me of the change. In order to compensate me and to stop
> my flood of protests, Laemmle, Junior, assigned me to
> adapt and direct Poe's Murders in the Rue Morgue.[21]

---

[19]Lugosi's biographer, Arthur Lennig, states Lugosi's
position in the following manner: "Lugosi, after the initial success of Dracula, was excited at last to be a big Hollywood star. He
saw himself as a sexy, romantic man who played the part of a vampire, and not a 'horror' man. Universal, on the other hand, felt
that Lugosi would be their new Lon Chaney. The former Hungarian
matinee idol was not entranced with the heavy make-up and love for
grotesquerie that marked Chaney's career" (Arthur Lennig, The
Count: The Life and Films of Bela "Dracula" Lugosi (New York:
G. P. Putnam's Sons, 1974), p. 115).

[20]Both Glut, The Frankenstein Legend, p. 93, and Jensen, Boris
Karloff, p. 24, state the major problem with the test was Lugosi's
make-up, which he modelled on Paul Wegener's in The Golem and
insisted on doing himself. The result was a complete failure.
Gifford, Karloff, pp. 39-40, agrees on the failure of the make-up,
but says Jack Pierce, not Lugosi, devised it.

[21]Florey, p. 164. The original French reads as follows: "James
Whale, l'as du Universal, demanda à Carl Laemmle de lui laisser
filmer Frankenstein, dont on m'avait promis la réalization. On donna
satisfaction a Whale, sans toutefois me mettre au courant de ce
changement. Pour me dédommager, et arrêter le flot de mes protestations, Laemmle Junior me chargea de l'adaptation et de la mise en
scène de Double assassinat dans la Rue Morgue après Poe." The
translation in the text is mine.

Whale himself said,

> I chose Frankenstein out of about thirty stories because
> it was the strongest meat and gave me a chance to dabble
> in the macabre . . . I thought it would be an amusing
> thing to try and make what everyone knows to be a physical
> impossibility into the almost believable for sixty minutes.
> Also, it offered fine pictorial chances, had two grand
> characterizations and had a subject that might go anywhere.[22]

At this time in 1931, Whale had directed only one picture for
Universal, Waterloo Bridge (Journey's End had been made for Tiffany-
Gainsborough), which had been a modest success (the New York Times
called it a "praiseworthy" picture),[23] and he was hardly in the
position to demand anything he wanted, Florey's designation of him
as the "ace of Universal" notwithstanding. Probably, Laemmle,
Junior, wanted Whale to direct Frankenstein because he desired a
British director for the job, and he had admired the way Whale had
conveyed "British atmosphere" in Waterloo Bridge.[24]

Originally, Laemmle had wanted Leslie Howard for the title role,
but Whale brought in his friend, Colin Clive, from Journey's End.
Bette Davis, who had appeared in Waterloo Bridge, was briefly
considered for the role of Elizabeth Frankenstein, but the more
established Mae Clarke got the part. Three other important roles
were filled by John Boles, Edward van Sloan, and Dwight Frye (van
Sloan and Frye had had major roles in Dracula), leaving only the
part of the Monster to be cast. For this all-important role,

---

[22]"James Whale and Frankenstein," New York Times, 20 December
1931, sect. 8, p. 4.

[23]Mordaunt Hall, "When Love is Blind: Waterloo Bridge," New
York Times, 5 September 1930, p. 7.

[24]Gifford, Karloff, pp. 37-38.

Whale selected a journeyman actor, forty-two years old, who had

already appeared in over sixty films since beginning his film career

in 1920.  His name was William Henry Pratt; his stage name was Boris

Karloff.[25]  According to Karloff, Whale simply approached him one

day at lunch in the Universal commissary and asked him to test for

the part.[26]

---

[25]The best book on Karloff is undoubtedly Paul Jensen, Boris
Karloff and His Films.  Denis Gifford, Karloff, provides good
information on the films, especially regarding cast lists, synopses,
and credits.  Peter Underwood, Karloff: The Life of Boris Karloff
(New York:  Drake Publishers, 1972), deals with the biographical
facts well, but makes no attempt to analyze the films.  Richard
Bojarski and Kenneth Beale, The Films of Boris Karloff (Secaucus,
N. J.:  Citadel Press, 1974), also contribute interesting back-
ground material on the films.  Of lesser value in every respect is
Cynthia Lindsay, Dear Boris:  The Life of William Henry Pratt,
A.K.A. Boris Karloff (New York:  Alfred A. Knopf, 1975).

[26]Lugosi's story that he recommended Karloff may, I think, be
safely considered a fabrication.  Over the years, Karloff has told
this story numerous times and, although there are minor alterations
in the various retellings, the main facts are always consistent.
See Beck, pp. 113-114; Brosnan, The Horror People, p. 44; Gifford,
Karloff, p. 39; Jensen, Boris Karloff, p. 24; and Lindsay, p. 54.
Karloff himself wrote of this momentous meeting in the following
manner:  "My big break came when I was downing a sandwich-and-tea
lunch in the Universal commissary.  After a string of sweet-and-
kindly roles, I had played the diabolical Galloway, the convict-
killer, in The Criminal Code.  Someone tapped me on the shoulder
and said, 'Mr. Whale would like to see you at his table.' . . .
'We're getting ready to shoot Frankenstein,' Whale said, 'and I'd
like you to test--for the part of the Monster.'  It was a bit
shattering, but I felt that any part was better than no part at
all" (Boris Karloff, "Memoirs of a Monster," Saturday Evening Post,
v. 235 (3 November 1962), p. 79).
     In an interview, Whale explained his reasons for choosing
Karloff.  "Boris Karloff's face had always fascinated me and I made
drawings of his head, adding sharp, bony ridges where I imagined
his skull might have been joined.  His physique was weaker than I
could wish, but that queer, penetrating personality of his, I felt,
was more important than his shape, which could easily be altered"
("James Whale and Frankenstein," New York Times, 20 December 1931,
sect. 8, p. 4).

The man responsible for Karloff's brilliant make-up was Jack
Pierce, an ex-professional baseball player, who headed Universal's
make-up department. Before designing the make-up, Pierce spent
several months researching the project. His description of his
work is not only interesting in its own right, but also demonstrates
the extraordinary patience and dedication of the Hollywood actors/
actresses and technicians of the studio years.

> My anatomical studies taught me that there are six ways
> a surgeon can cut the skull in order to take out or put
> in a brain. I figured that Frankenstein, who was a
> scientist, but no practicing surgeon, would take the
> simplest surgical way. He would cut the top of the skull
> off straight across like a pot-lid, hinge it, pop the
> brain in, and then clamp it on tight. That is the reason
> I decided to make the Monster's head square and flat like
> a shoe box, and dig that big scar across his forehead
> with the metal clamps holding it together.
> Those two metal studs sticking out of the Monster's
> neck . . . are inlets for electricity. . . . Remember,
> the Monster is an electrical gadget. So Karloff . . .
> carries a five-pound steel spine . . . to represent the
> rod which conveys the current up to the Monster's brain.
> I read that the Egyptians used to bind some crimi-
> nals hand and foot and bury them alive. When their blood
> turned to water after death, it flowed into their extrem-
> ities, stretched their arms to gorilla length, and swelled
> their hands, feet and faces to abnormal proportions. I
> thought this might make a nice touch for the Monster. . . .
> So I fixed him up that way. Those lizard eyes of his are
> rubber, like his false head. I made his arms look longer
> by shortening the sleeves of his coat, stiffened his legs
> with two pairs of pants over steel struts, and by means
> of asphalt walker's boots gave him those Newfoundland dogs.
> I cover Karloff's face with blue-green greasepaint which
> photographs gray. I blacken his fingernails with shoe
> polish. It takes me four hours to build him up every
> morning and two hours to tear him down every night.[27]

---

[27]"Oh, You Beautiful Monster," New York Times, 29 January 1939,
sect. 9, p. 4.

As Carl Laemmle, Junior, aptly understated, "Karloff's eyes
mirrored the suffering we needed."[28]

Frankenstein was shot in August-September of 1931 and released
in December.  Before its final release, two important changes were made.
The more serious, artistically, was the cut in the sequence where the
Monster accidentally drowns the little girl, Maria.  The other
revision provided for a happy ending by allowing Henry Frankenstein
to live, rather than die as he was slated to do in the original script.

Although Karloff insisted that he was the instigator of the
cut in the drowning scene,[29] Laemmle, Junior, was almost certainly
the perpetrator.  He became alarmed when the film was previewed in
Santa Barbara because a large number of the audience, apparently in
reaction to the violence and Karloff's horrifying make-up, walked
out.[30]  This so concerned Laemmle that he made the cut and ordered
the ending revised.  He need not have worried.  Financially,
Frankenstein became one of the most successful films of all time.
It was made for approximately $250,000 and eventually grossed about
$13,000,000.[31]  In comparison, Star Wars, the highest grossing

---

[28]Underwood, p. 67.

[29]Beck, pp. 114-115, and Glut, The Frankenstein Legend,
pp. 112-114.

[30]Underwood, p. 68.

[31]Many sources verify these general figures.  See Brosnan, The
Horror People, p. 47; Gifford, Karloff, p. 49; and Glut, The Frankenstein
Legend, p. 120.

movie ever, was made for $9,500,000[32] and, as of August, 1978, had grossed $258,000,000,[33] a highly respectable return of more than twenty-five times its production cost. However, Frankenstein has returned more than fifty times its production cost!

The critics immediately realized that Frankenstein was a different kind of film, but the source of its powerful effect eluded them. The New York Times commented on the "disturbing nature" of this "artistically conceived work,"[34] and the New York Daily News stated that it was a tale which "clutches at you icily and holds you."[35] Even the jaded audience of Hollywood was jolted. The talented screenwriter, Frances Marion (Dinner at Eight, The Champ, Camille), wrote in her autobiography that it was "a curious fact, but scarcely anyone young or old in the audience viewed the picture without some nerve-tingling reaction."[36] It is now appropriate to explore the reasons for this "nerve-tingling reaction" produced by Frankenstein.

---

[32]"Star Wars: The Year's Best Movie," Time, v. 109 (30 May 1977), p. 61.

[33]Bill O'Hallaren, "Behind the Scenes at Battlestar Galactica," TV Guide, v. 26 (16 September 1978), p. 34.

[34]Mordaunt Hall, "Frankenstein," New York Times, 5 December 1931, p. 21.

[35]Quoted in Bojarski and Beale, p. 63.

[36]Frances Marion, Off With Their Heads! A Serio-Comic Tale of Hollywood (New York: Macmillan Publishing Co., 1972), p. 231.

## Analysis:  Frankenstein

Henry Frankenstein (Colin Clive) is a young scientist obsessed
with the desire to create life.  Aided by his hunchbacked assistant,
Fritz (Dwight Frye), he robs graves to obtain needed body organs.
Instructed to steal a brain, Fritz mistakenly takes an "abnormal"
one.  Alarmed by Henry's condition, his fiancée, Elizabeth (Mae
Clarke), best friend, Victor Moritz (John Boles), and ex-professor,
Dr. Waldman (Edward van Sloan), visit his laboratory on the very
night that Henry is planning his grand experiment.  During a raging
storm, Henry successfully harnesses electrical energy and creates
an artificial man (Boris Karloff).  The Monster is kept in a dungeon,
where Fritz tortures him with torches and whips.  Breaking free, the
Monster kills Fritz and is subdued by Waldman and Henry.  After this
incident, Henry collapses and is taken home by his father, Baron
Frankenstein (Frederick Kerr), and Elizabeth, leaving Waldman to
cope with the Monster.  On Henry's wedding day, the Monster strangles
Dr. Waldman and escapes.  He accidentally drowns a little girl, Maria
(Marilyn Harris), and enters the Frankenstein mansion where he confronts Elizabeth, but does not harm her.  Henry joins the villagers
in hunting for the Monster.  During the hunt, the Monster encounters
Henry alone, overpowers him, and carries him to an abandoned windmill.  Henry and the Monster fight on the roof and Henry is hurled
to the ground.  The villagers set fire to the windmill and burn it
down, supposedly destroying the Monster.  In the film's original
ending, Henry dies also, but, in the altered version, he lives.

The primary governing pattern of <u>Frankenstein</u> is Whale's light-darkness contrast and his alliance of fire with this contrast.[37] The film proper[38] opens during a funeral in a graveyard at dusk. The somber tone is set at once. At first, the screen is blank and only the sound of weeping is heard on the sound track. Then, while a priest intones a prayer for the dead in the background, the camera focuses on the hands of the gravedigger as he lowers the coffin into the grave and slowly pans over the faces of the mourners, coming to rest on a statue of Death. A tolling bell is heard in the distance. As the weeping figures leave, the gravedigger begins to shovel dirt into the grave. The only sound is the ominous thudding of the dirt onto the coffin. The weeping, the prayer, the tolling bell, and the sound of the dirt are aural symbols of death which complement the visual symbols of the graveyard, the statue of Death, the darkness, and the coffin. Fire becomes allied to death when the gravedigger, his task completed, strikes a match to light his pipe. But fire does not represent only death; it is also a symbol of life, for Henry uses Heavenly fire, lightning, to create the Monster. Like Whale's other major symbolic element, hands, fire carries both positive and negative connotations: it may create or it may destroy.

---

[37]For many of the ideas associated with the motifs of light, darkness, and fire, I am especially indebted to R. H. W. Dillard, <u>Horror Films</u> (New York: Monarch Press, 1976), pp. 13-28.

[38]There is a prologue during which Edward van Sloan steps from behind a curtain and warns the audience that this tale "may shock you. It might even horrify you."

When the gravedigger leaves the cemetery, Henry and Fritz enter to steal the body. Henry wears partially light clothes (a white shirt), Fritz wears dark ones, thus tying Fritz more closely to the death-darkness motif than Henry. Later in the film, when Fritz enters the brightly-lit lecture hall in his dark clothes to steal the brain, he passes his hand in front of his face twice, as if to ward off the light. Significantly, Henry and Fritz are introduced by moonlight while Elizabeth and Victor are introduced by the artificial light of candles and lamps, "fire tamed to civilized uses,"[39] making them representatives of ordinary life and light, as opposed to Henry's identification with death and darkness. Although R. H. W. Dillard says that Dr. Waldman is also introduced by lamp-light,[40] he is actually first seen under an _electric_ light, the highest form of artificial light, allying him with "white" or "good" science in contrast to Henry's practice of "black" or "bad" science. In a conversation with Dr. Waldman, Henry says that he wants to find the secret of what "changes _darkness_ into _light_" and, in the first part of the film, he is groping through a metaphorical darkness (scientific ignorance) toward what he considers the higher light of scientific knowledge (the creation of life). However, in the process of his quest, he forgets that, in common with all men, he possesses a dark side. Like Jim in Joseph Conrad's _Lord Jim_, Henry is unprepared to deal with this darkness.

---

[39]Dillard, _Horror Films_, p. 16.

[40]Ibid.

The pattern of light, fire, and darkness continues throughout
the film. Fire as a life-giving force is demonstrated in the
powerful creation scene. In this sequence, Henry resembles Captain
Ahab in Herman Melville's Moby Dick, as he defies the lightning by
capturing its creative principle (fire) and bringing his own creation
to life. Just as Ahab grasps the main-mast links during the typhoon,
Henry grips the controls of his laboratory apparatus while the
lightning crackles menacingly overhead. Implicitly, Henry echoes
Ahab's shout to the heavens, "I now know thy right worship is defiance."[41]
Robert Zoellner's "entropic paradigm," which he applies to Ahab, of
"light coming out of darkness doomed to return to darkness"[42] works
as well for Henry. From out of the darkness of the storm comes the
creative force of lightning, "the most active and meaningful fusion
of light and fire,"[43] to bring into existence a creature of darkness
(the Monster is always dressed in dark clothes), who is doomed to
return to the darkness of the grave from whence he came.

The Monster's fear of fire is closely tied, first, to his violent
origins, and, second, to the Promethean overtones of the film. Born
in a traumatic flashing of fire and light, the Monster seems to

---

[41] Herman Melville, Moby Dick (New York: Holt, Rinehart, and
Winston, 1948), p. 498.

[42] Robert Zoellner, The Salt-Sea Mastodon: A Reading of Moby
Dick (Berkeley and Los Angeles: University of California Press,
1973), p. 197.

[43] Dillard, Horror Films, p. 18.

subconsciously remember the shock of his birth and the fire's role in that birth. In addition, Henry is, as the subtitle of the novel states, a modern Prometheus. According to Greek mythology, Prometheus created man and, realizing that he was inferior to the animals in strength and cunning, stole fire from Heaven for man's protection.[44] Prometheus also taught man the arts of Hephaestus and Athena, which included agriculture and handicrafts.[45] Henry steals fire from Heaven to create life, but he uses the fire to control the Monster, not to protect him. Unlike Prometheus, Henry is not interested in teaching the Monster; his great goal, laudable enough in theory, is to do something no man has ever done--create life. But he is unprepared to deal with the results of his creation. He is, as Richard Chase notes of Ahab, a false Prometheus.[46] Prometheus, a God himself, provided a "divine spark" to create man, but Henry, a mortal, cannot provide such a "spark" for the Monster, and the Monster recognizes that he is not God-made but man-made.[47] Thus,

---

[44]Apollodorus, Gods and Heroes of the Greeks: The Library of Apollodorus, trans. Michael Simpson (Amherst, Mass.: University of Massachusetts Press, 1976), p. 32.

[45]Plato, "Protagoras," in The Dialogues of Plato, 4th edition, v. I, trans. B. Jowett (Oxford: The Clarendon Press, 1953), pp. 146-147.

[46]Richard Chase, Herman Melville: A Critical Study (New York: Macmillan Publishing Co., 1949), p. 47.

[47]As the Monster develops intellectually, he becomes conscious of his origins. In The Bride of Frankenstein, when Dr. Pretorius asks him if he knows who he is and who Henry is, the Monster replies, "Yes. Made me from dead."

fire, to the Monster, does not represent divinity, but his human, non-divine origins, and this knowledge is reflected in his fear of fire.

Visually, the creation scene is notable for its pictorial depiction of the Monster as a new Adam. As the table on which the Monster is strapped is lowered to the floor, Whale cuts to a close-up of his hand, hanging in a limp, flexed position, remarkably similar to the position of Adam's hand in Michelangelo's painting, "The Creation of Adam," on the Sistine Chapel ceiling. But it is not God's hand that has animated the Monster, but man's in the person of Henry Frankenstein. And Henry is not a rational, but a crazed, pseudo-God; as the Monster's hand moves indicating life, Henry screams repeatedly, "It's alive! It's alive!"[48] This "Adam" will never inhabit a Garden of Eden, but a world of pain and fear.

An excellent example of Whale's use of the light-dark opposition (and of his fluid editing style) occurs in the famous scene of the Monster's first appearance. A shot analysis of this scene follows:[49]

Setting: Henry Frankenstein's laboratory. Henry and Dr.
         Waldman are present.

---

[48]In a scene deleted from the present version, Henry's God-like aspirations are explicitly noted. As he screams, "It's alive! It's alive!" Victor rushes to him and says, "Henry, in the name of God!" Henry replies, "Oh, God--Now I know what it feels like to be God."

[49]There is no standardized format for a shot-by-shot analysis. I have elected to follow the method employed by Roy Huss, "Almost Eve: The Creation Scene in The Bride of Frankenstein," in Focus on the Horror Film, eds. Roy Huss and T. J. Ross (Englewood Cliffs, N. J.: Prentice-Hall, 1972), pp. 74-82.

Shot No.
1. Long shot of a door.  The door opens and the Monster
   backs into the room.

Cut to:
2. Medium shot of the Monster.  His back is still turned.
   Slowly, he turns to his left to face the camera.

Quick cut to:
3. Close-up of the Monster's face from his neck up.

Quick cut to:
4. Extreme close-up of the Monster.  His face fills the
   screen.  During this series of cuts, there is total
   silence on the sound track.

Comment: Despite the overfamiliarity of the Monster today,
this sequence of shots remains, as Drake Douglas
says, "one of the most frightening moments in screen
history."[50]  In Ivan Butler's words, Karloff's
"gaunt features and dark socketed eyes  have a true
charnel-house appearance."[51]  This stylistic technique of introducing a main character by means of
extremely quick cuts is one which Whale will repeat
in his other horror films.  The extreme close-up
serves to shock the audience, to emphasize the
profound isolation of the Monster (a theme which is
also important in Bride and The Invisible Man), and
to indicate the general feeling of claustrophobia
and enclosure which is so important to an effective
horror film.

Cut to:
5. Long shot of the Monster.  Henry approaches from the
   left and faces the Monster.  He beckons the Monster
   toward him.

   Henry:  "Come in, come in."

   Henry backs away to the right and the camera pans with
   him.  He stops before a chair and motions for the
   Monster to sit.

---

[50]Drake Douglas, Horror! (New York:  Collier Books, 1966),
p. 112.

[51]Butler, p. 48.

Henry:  "Sit down, sit down."

The Monster obeys.

Henry (to Waldman):  "You see, it understands.  Watch."

Cut to:
6.  Low angle long shot of a shuttered skylight.  Henry opens the skylight.

Cut to:
7.  Medium shot of the Monster on the chair.  Slowly, the light from the skylight crosses his face.

Cut to:
8.  Close-up of the Monster's face.  He raises his head slowly and begins to rise.

Cut to:
9.  Medium long shot of the Monster.  He rises, still looking up, moves jerkily forward, and raises his hands toward the light.

Cut to:
10.  Medium close-up of the Monster's head and upraised arms.

Waldman:  "Shut off the light!"

The Monster tries to "catch" the light in his hands. Henry closes the skylight.  The Monster lowers his hands.

Comment:  Significantly, it is Henry, at Waldman's urging, who shuts out the light.  Whale implies that, in spite of the Monster's dark beginnings, he might be able to lead a normal life, to reach the light, if man would only give him a chance.

Cut to:
11.  Medium long shot which includes all three characters. The Monster gestures helplessly at Henry.

Henry:  "Sit down.  Go and sit down."

The Monster backs to the chair and sits.

Cut to:
12.  Close-up of the Monster's yearning face.  The camera tilts down to his futilely gesturing hands.

This entire sequence is masterfully done. The light serves as a "symbol of reason and grace from which he [the Monster] is forever barred"[52] because mankind will not allow him an opportunity of "catch" the sunlight; the Monster becomes an "emblem of fallen and unredeemeed man";[53] and the scene as a whole "brilliantly characterizes the Monster and functions as a small scale allegory of man's efforts to grasp the intangible unknown and of his bewilderment at a Creator who keeps him from it."[54] Typically, Whale also uses this scene for emotional effect by leaving one unsure of what to think or feel. One's first reaction is revulsion, for the Monster is truly a thing of death, a "charnel-house" being, but the revulsion changes to sad sympathy because he is also pathetic in his helpless, questing innocence, expressively and eloquently articulated by his gesturing hands.

Immediately after this sequence, Fritz enters brandishing a torch, and the Monster is conveyed back to the dungeon, where Fritz tortures him with the torch and a whip. The dungeon set and lighting are pure Expressionism (as is Henry's laboratory, aptly described as "a jumbled collection of massive off-plumb walls, crazily tilted beams, and oddly-cut windows")[55] composed of

---

[52] John Baxter, Sixty Years of Hollywood (New York: A. S. Barnes, 1973), p. 90.

[53] Dillard, Horror Films, p. 19.

[54] Jensen, Boris Karloff, p. 31.

[55] Tropp, p. 87.

weirdly askew walls and slanted windows, without a single right
angle. In the background is a small barred window, through which
rays of sunlight struggle to enter, but they cannot reach the
Monster. The only time that the Monster walks in sunlight results in catastrophe: the drowning of Maria. The drowning is
not the Monster's fault, but the consequence of Henry's shirking
of responsibility for his creation. The Monster, dimly intuiting
that water is the natural antagonist of the fearful fire, naturally
regards the lake as an unmitigated good. He has never been taught
that water can kill, and the price of his knowledge is the death
of little Maria.

The pattern of light and dark continues in the scenes at
Baron Frankenstein's mansion. Although Martin Tropp says these
scenes "seem dragged in for no purpose whatsoever,"[56] their in-
tent is quite clear and very effective, namely, to contrast the
"serenity of the real world with the nightmare world of labora-
tories, gibbets, and graveyards."[57] The Baron represents the
status quo. His house is filled with light (significantly,
candlelight and lamplight, not electric light; the Baron is no
believer in science), not darkness. When Elizabeth and Victor
try to explain Henry's prolonged absence as being due to his
experiments, the Baron's reaction is immediate and conventional:
"There's another woman and you're afraid to tell me. Pretty sort
of experiments these must be." Despite the staid orthodoxy of the

---

[56]Ibid., p. 93.

[57]Everson, Classics of the Horror Film, p. 45.

53

Baron's attitudes, there is something reassuring about his common-
places when set against what are obviously acts of madness in
Henry's "nightmare world."

The most brightly lit scene in the film occurs at the Baron's
after Henry has been brought home. Henry and Elizabeth are relaxing
on the terrace, talking of their approaching wedding. But, as
Dillard notes, fire--and, therefore, danger--are present even in
this peaceful scene, since Henry is smoking a cigarette.[58] Further,
as Henry leans over to kiss Elizabeth, the smoke from his cigarette drifts between them. Thus, the fire figuratively divides
them even in the safety and comfort of the fixed social order which
is the Baron's world. Even as Henry and Elizabeth kiss, the Monster
is walking in the sunlight toward his fateful encounter with Maria, and,
in a masterful stroke of editing, Whale unites these two scenes.
He cuts away from Henry and Elizabeth to the wedding celebration in
the village. The camera begins a tracking movement through the
frolicking villagers while lively dance music reverberates on the
sound track. Suddenly, there is a quick cut to the Monster walking
in the woods. The camera movement remains the same, tracking along
with the Monster, but the polka music is replaced by the foreboding
sound of the Monster crashing through the underbrush. Deftly,
Whale makes the point that even in the midst of light and life, darkness and death are never far away.

---

[58]Dillard, Horror Films, p. 22.

As the film progresses, the Monster grows stronger and
stronger, particularly (and appropriately) at night. Just before Dr. Waldman is about to begin his dissection, he notes in
his journal that it is becoming increasingly difficult to keep
the Monster under sedation. Significantly, the time is 7:30 p.m.,
twilight. Waldman has waited too long; the Monster revives and
strangles him. The final pursuit of the Monster takes place at
night and, during this pursuit, he confronts Henry alone. Brushing
aside Henry's symbol of power and authority, the torch, the Monster
easily overpowers him. The ending of the film brings together the
fire, darkness, and light motifs. Light is noticeable by its absence,
for the climax occurs, fittingly, at night; the Monster was created
from the darkness and is returned to the darkness, In another
suitable image, the scene is lit only by the fire from the villagers'
torches; fire was responsible for the Monster's birth, and it is
now the cause of his death.

Fire, light, and darkness are the most important symbolic
elements in Frankenstein, but they are certainly not the only ones.
Whale's use of flowers, dogs, and, especially, hands also deserves
examination.

Flowers function in the first part of the film as symbols
of beauty, life, and happiness. The Baron's home is filled with
flowers, the Burgomaster brings a bouquet to Elizabeth, and the street
are decorated with flowers for the wedding festivities. Flowers
also represent tradition and continuity; the orange blossoms which
Henry and Victor wear for the wedding have been preserved in the

during the Monster's encounter with Maria.  In her childish
innocence, Maria has no fear of the Monster; she only wants
him to play with her.  They throw flowers into the water and
watch them float.  Maria shares her flowers with the Monster,
and, from this point to the end of the film, flowers are associated with ugliness, death, and sorrow rather than beauty, life,
and happiness.[59]  After throwing in all the flowers, the Monster
throws Maria into the lake, hoping to see her float also, but,
instead, she drowns.  The scene as it now stands ends with the Monster
reaching out for Maria.  This notorious excision is truly a terrible
mistake.[60]  The scene, apparently cut because Laemmle, Junior, considered it too violent, now connotes a crime of sexual perversion,
since the next sequence shows Maria's father carrying the bedraggled

---

[59]Whale's use of a shifting symbol is analogous to James Joyce's
use of the bird-flight motif in A Portrait of the Artist as a
Young Man (New York: Viking Press, 1964).  Initially, birds and
flight symbolize Stephen Dedaulus' sense of fear and guilt--"a
heavy bird flying low through the grey light" (Joyce, p. 22);
later, birds and flight represent Stephen's feeling of freedom
and happiness--"a hawklike man flying sunward above the sea"
(Joyce, p. 169).

[60]According to Glut, The Frankenstein Legend, p. 113, and
Jensen, Boris Karloff, p. 38, eight shots are missing from the scene.
They both reproduce material from a cutting-continuity script,
which I assume they obtained either from Universal Studios or
the Academy of Motion Picture Arts and Sciences, but, since they
do not document their source, I cannot be sure.  My attempts to
acquire copies of the script were thwarted by copyright restrictions.
According to Glut, The Frankenstein Legend, p. 113, the footage
is available in "certain re-release prints," but Richard Anobile,
James Whale's Frankenstein (New York:  Universe Books, 1974), p.
6, was unable to obtain the footage while preparing his shot-by-
shot reconstruction of Frankenstein and theorizes that the missing
frames no longer exist.

body of the dead child through the village. Thus, the emotional effect
works against the sympathy and pathos which Whale has carefully built
up for the Monster.[61]  Ivan Butler, who has seen the missing portion,
says, "Karloff's final departure, wringing his hands in an agony of
dawning comprehension, is as moving a moment as any on the screen."[62]
However, if the drowning scene is marred, the episode which follows
definitely is not. The walk of Maria's father through the village with
the dead girl in his arms is an exact and artful reversal of the previous
camera track through the celebrating villagers.  In the earlier sequence,
the camera movement was from screen left to screen right;

---

[61]Karloff steadfastly maintained that he insisted the cut be
made and Calvin Thomas Beck, pp. 114-115, records how Karloff explained his reasoning:  "'That was the only time when I didn't like
Jimmy Whale's direction.  We were on our knees opposite each other
when the moment came that there were no more flowers.  My conception
of the scene was that the Monster would look up at the little girl
in bewilderment and, in his mind, she would become a flower.  Without moving, he would pick her up gently and put her in the water
exactly as he had done the flowers--and, to his horror, she would
sink.  Well, Jimmy wanted me to do that,' Karloff motioned violently
over his head with both hands, 'over my head, which became a brutal
and deliberate act.  By no stretch of the imagination could you
make that innocent.  The whole pathos of the scene, to my mind,
should have been . . . completely innocent and unaware.  But the
moment you do that,' he motioned again with his arms, 'it's a
deliberate thing; and I insisted on that part being removed.'" (Beck's
emphasis)  As I have noted above, Laemmle almost surely removed the
frames for his own reasons, although Karloff probably thought his
opinion mattered.  In retrospect, it appears fortunate that any of
the scene was retained, since Karloff indicates that everyone except
Whale opposed Maria's death.  In an interview shortly before his
death, Karloff quotes Whale as follows:  "'The death has to take
place,' he [Whale] said.  He fumbled for his words as he tried to
convey why to us, because in a strange way we were all very hostile
about it. . . . And I think we understood why then, although I don't
now" (Tom Hutchinson, Horror and Fantasy in the Movies (New York:
Crescent Books, 1974), p. 42). (Hutchinson's emphasis)

[62]Butler, p. 41.

now the movement is from right to left along the same route. As
Maria's father passes each group of jubilant townspeople, the
dancing and music gradually cease until there is total silence on
the sound track.

With the shift in symbolic context, the flower-bedecked halls
of the Baron's mansion become an ill omen. After Elizabeth tells
Henry of her fear that "something is coming between us," she picks
up a bouquet and paces back and forth in her bedroom. Suddenly,
the Monster enters and confronts her. When Henry and Victor, respondin
to her screams, burst in, Elizabeth has fainted and the flowers
are strewn all over the room. Whale uses this reversal of flowers'
traditional symbolic meaning to graphically demonstrate that the
Monster, a creature of ugliness and death, cannot be joined to
beauty and life. Also, the impossibility of the Monster having a
"normal" emotional relationship with women is conveyed by Maria's
drowning and the frightening of Elizabeth. The Monster is thus
totally alone and isolated, incapable of surviving in a society
which places so much value on outward signs of transient beauty
(e.g., flowers) and "normal" male-female (i.e., handsome man-
beautiful woman) relationships.

In addition to flowers, Whale's use of dogs is interesting
and effective. In the opening graveyard scene, the baying of
dogs is heard in the distance, associating them with death and
darkness, and with the unnatural experiments of Henry Frankenstein.
The dogs' persistent howling throughout the film becomes emble-
matic of the abnormality of Henry's ideas. While Henry and

Elizabeth talk on the terrace, two large dogs lie at their feet,
apparent representatives of the security and material comfort of
the Baron's world.  However, due to the dogs' earlier associations,
their presence in the scene, like the smoke from Henry's cigarette,
strikes a note of foreboding.  In the final pursuit of the Monster,
the yelping of the dogs is constantly heard, as they become figuratively "hounds of Hell" (emphasized by several close-ups of the
hounds) chasing the Monster to his doom.

Throughout Frankenstein (and Bride), an important recurring
motif is Whale's use of hands.  The first shot in the film is a
close-up of the gravedigger's hands lowering the coffin into the
grave and, shortly afterward, Henry's hands are highlighted as he
raises the casket from the grave.  These two early instances form
a prolepsis of the way hands will be used in the film, that is,
as agents of destruction and creation.  As with fire, hands have
both positive and negative connotations.

In the creation scene, the first indication that the Monster
is alive comes when he moves his right hand.  This movement is
exactly repeated when Dr. Waldman is about to dissect the Monster,
but it now becomes a movement of death (Waldman is strangled), not
life.

Hands as instruments of creation are emphasized when Henry
stares at his hands prior to the Monster's creation and says,
"The brain of a dead man waiting to live again in a body I made with
my own hands.  With my own hands."  Likewise, hands as implements
of destruction are stressed when, just before setting out to hunt

down the Monster, Henry states, "I made him with these hands and with these hands, I will destroy him."

In the scene with Maria, her hands represent light and life, while the Monster's signify darkness and death. Briefly, the creature of darkness is joined to the sunlight world by touching hands with Maria. But this link, as fragile as the flowers which Maria hands the Monster, is soon broken, for man denies the Monster entrance to the light world.

Whale also uses hands to express certain character traits, a method often effectively employed in literature.[63] In this respect, Henry and the Monster are similar to Wing Biddlebaum in Sherwood Anderson's "Hands." Due to a traumatic, unjustified, child-molester charge in his youth, Biddlebaum is an emotional cripple. Although his hands have remarkable dexterity (he can pick up bread crumbs and carry "them to his mouth one by one with remarkable rapidity"),[64] he is unable to use them to communicate his emotions and feelings, fearing that his actions will be misinterpreted. Whenever his gestures become too expressive, he tries to hide his hands in his pockets or behind his back. When Henry first considers his creation of the Monster, he looks at his hands with awe and pride,

---

[63]A good example is Charles Dickens' Great Expectations. Pip is first made aware of his inferior social status by Estella's comments about his rough hands; Jaggers' use of his hands conveys his air of authority and dominance; and Joe's hands are dexterous when he is comfortable in his blacksmith's shop, but clumsy when he is ill at ease in Pip's London apartment.

[64]Sherwood Anderson, "Hands," in Winesburg, Ohio (New York: Viking Press, 1958), p. 34.

but, after Elizabeth has been attacked, he speaks of them with fear and loathing as if, like Wing Biddlebaum's hands, they had betrayed him. Since the Monster is mute, his hands are virtually his sole means of communication and, although they "speak" eloquently, this is overlooked by Henry, Waldman, and others who see only the ugliness of his face and figure. Thus, the Monster too, in his inability to convey his feelings, is linked to Biddlebaum.

This idea of linking and joining is also explored by Whale in his employment of linked or paired characters. The two most obviously paired characters in Frankenstein are Henry and Fritz. In a very real sense, Fritz is a part of Henry, an "embodiment of his twisted emotions."[65] At the beginning of the film, as Fritz rises to look over the cemetery fence, Henry, as if speaking to himself, cries, "Down, down, you fool!" Henry uses Fritz as his arms and legs, while he (Henry) supplies the intellect. Only in the opening sequence does Henry join in any physical labor, the robbing of the grave. Afterwards, he has Fritz cut down the hanged man, sends him to steal the brain, and repeatedly orders him to scurry up and down the laboratory stairs. In three instances, Fritz can be seen looking through barred enclosures, symbolically trying to break free of Henry's mind: in the opening scene, he peers through the cemetery fence railing; before breaking into the lecture hall, he is seen watching through the window; and,

---

[65]Tropp, p. 91.

when Elizabeth, Victor, and Dr. Waldman come to the laboratory, he
opens the door and gazes at them through a narrow grating. When
Fritz is killed by the Monster, Henry collapses and Waldman, in
an amusing and suggestive line, tells him, "Come, pull yourself
together." But, when Victor, Elizabeth, and the Baron arrive, Henry
breaks down again and mumbles deliriously over and over, "My poor
Fritz, my poor Fritz." The most convincing evidence that Fritz is
a part of Henry occurs just prior to the creation scene. Arranging
the situation for the maximum theatrical effect, Henry seats Elizabeth, Victor, and Dr. Waldman in a semicircle to watch his bravura
performance. Victor has just called Henry "crazy," and he now
responds, "Quite a good scene, isn't it? One man crazy, three very
sane spectators." However, there are clearly _four_, not three, spectators. Henry has forgotten Fritz, his embodied demon; the dark
side of his personality has broken free and is no longer under his
control (significantly, when Henry tells Fritz to stop tormenting
the Monster with fire, Fritz disobeys).

Henry is also joined to his creation, the Monster. The tie
between the Monster and Henry is, of course, subject to a Freudian
interpretation. Although I do not intend to deal with specific
Freudian implications in Frankenstein, it should be noted that
other critics have done so. For instance, Margaret Tarratt sees
the Monster as the personification of Henry's "repressed sexual

desires, the impulses of the id,"[66] and thinks that Henry's sexual
drive is the "estranging factor" between him and Elizabeth.[67]
Walter Evans believes that the Monster is an "embodiment of Frankenstein's sexuality"[68] and that, in order to enter into a normal
sexual relationship with Elizabeth, Henry must give up his
"dangerous private experiments" (i.e., masturbation).[69] Evans'
general theory on the appeal of horror movies is that they "mirror
the sexual traumas of adolescence,"[70] and fulfill adolescents'
"need for rituals of initiation, and for puberty rituals specif-
ically."[71] Harvey Greenberg states that the real purpose of Henry's
investigations is "the resolution of his sexual ignorance and angst,"[72]
and that his research, entered into because he is afraid of a
sexual relationship with Elizabeth, is a "masturbatory metaphor."[73]
For Greenberg, the "appeal of the monster movie may, at least in

---

[66]Margaret Tarratt, "Monsters From the Id," in Film Genre:
Theory and Criticism, ed. Barry K. Grant (Metuchen, N. J.:
Scarecrow Press, 1977), p. 168.

[67]Ibid., pp. 173-174.

[68]Walter Evans, "Monster Movies: A Sexual Theory,"
Journal of Popular Film, v. 2 (Fall 1973), p. 359.

[69]Ibid.

[70]Walter Evans, "Monster Movies and Rites of Initiation,"
Journal of Popular Film, v. 4 (Spring 1975), p. 124.

[71]Ibid., p. 137.

[72]Harvey Greenberg, The Movies On Your Mind (New York:
Saturday Review Press, 1975), p. 208.

[73]Ibid., p. 209.

63

part, be traced to our fascination with the child-like innocence of these fearsome creatures."[74]

Whether or not one accepts a Freudian critical position, it is undeniable that, as in the novel, creator and creation are inextricably linked.[75] Henry recognizes this when he states, "I made him with these _hands_ and with these _hands_, I will destroy him." As Henry faces his creation alone on the mountain, their unity is shown in a four-shot sequence: a medium shot of Henry is followed by a medium shot of the Monster, then a close-up of Henry is followed by a close-up of the Monster. The shots are of the same duration and the two characters have the same expression on their faces. Later, in the windmill, Whale uses the same technique to stress the bond between them. Alternating shots show Henry and the Monster staring at each other through the turning gear of the windmill. Once again, their expressions are identical. In these scenes, Whale vividly demonstrates that the Monster is Henry's Doppelgänger, his "double."

---

[74]Ibid., p. 213.

[75]That the Monster and his creator are linked in the novel was first implicitly recognized by Eino Railo, The Haunted Castle: A Study of the Elements of English Romanticism (London: George Routledge and Sons, 1927), pp. 311-312, and Richard Church, Mary Shelley (London: Gerald Howe, 1928), p. 54. More explicit discussions of this point may be found in Harold Bloom, "Frankenstein, or the Modern Prometheus: A Review," Partisan Review, v. 32 (Fall 1965), pp. 611-618; Lowry Nelson, Jr., "Night Thoughts on the Gothic Novel," Yale Review, v. 52 (December 1952), pp. 243-248; Muriel Spark, Child of Light: A Reassessment of Mary Wollstonecraft Shelley (Hadleigh, Essex, Eng.: Tower Bridge Publishers, 1951), pp. 134-149; and William Walling, Mary Shelley (New York: Twayne, 1972), pp. 39-40.

An important thematic element, one which is developed more fully in Bride, is religious and Christian symbolism. For instance, the opening grave-robbing scene is clearly meant to be a reverse (and perverse) Resurrection. As Henry and Fritz enter the cemetery, they pass between a large cross serving as a grave marker, a statue of Death, and a statue of the crucified Christ. As they begin to work, the cross and the Death statue are seen in the background. Then one of their shovels is placed vertically in the ground and a coat and hat are hung on it. As the coffin is raised, Henry pulls a stake from the grave and plants it at a horizontal angle to the shovel, thus forming another cross. Now, the grave marker cross is on the left of the screen, the shovel and the stake are in the center, and the statue of Death is on the right. The coffin stands in a tilted upright position and Whale cuts to a close-up of Henry gripping the casket. He says, "He's just resting, waiting for a new life to come." The scene becomes an echo of the Crucifixion, a parody of the Resurrection, and a subtle burlesque of the Trinity. In Bride, this religious parallel is strengthened as the Monster is explicitly identified with Christ.

Since Carlos Clarens describes Frankenstein as a film "unrelieved by humor,"[76] a word should be said about Whale's use of comedy. Certainly, the comic scenes in Frankenstein are not comparable to the sophisticated black humor of Bride, or the sardonic dialogue of The Invisible Man, but the film is not totally devoid

---

[76]Clarens, An Illustrated History, p. 63.

of light moments. For example, at the beginning of the film, as
Henry digs feverishly in the grave, he throws a spadeful of dirt
directly into the face of the statue of Death. This shot is not
only humorous, but also reinforces the idea of a reverse Resurrection.

All the Baron's scenes provide contrast and relief from the
somberness of the graveyard and laboratory scenes. His previously
mentioned discussion with Elizabeth and Victor in which he believes
Henry's absence to be due to "another woman," his scene with the
Burgomaster ("Nothing the Burgomaster has to say can be of the
slightest importance"), and his reaction at seeing a burning torch
on the floor of Henry's watchtower laboratory ("What a forsaken
place. Are you trying to burn it down?") exemplify the comic relief
provided by the Baron.

Even Fritz is used for humorous purposes, albeit in a more
farcical manner. In the brain-stealing scene, he runs into a
jangling skeleton and is so shocked by the sound of a gong that he
drops the "normal" brain and is forced to substitute an "abnormal"
one.[77]

The most wryly amusing scene is Whale's "grotesque variation"
on the "knocking at the gate" episode from Macbeth (Act II,

---

[77]Without doubt, this scene is the weakest in the film. Conceived by Florey, p. 164, it appears to have been retained by Whale
because he had a liking for broad comedy (as evidenced by the scenes
with Una O'Connor in Bride and The Invisible Man) as well as subtle,
sophisticated humor. Fortunately, Whale's direction and Karloff's
acting stress motivations such as fear of the unknown, a desire for
self-preservation, and the problem of a new mind in a fully-grown
body--rather than the influence of an "abnormal" brain--for the
Monster's actions. Still, the scene could have been cut with no
loss to the film.

scene iii).[78]  Both scenes take place at night; the setting for
Macbeth is a castle, for Frankenstein a castle-like watchtower.  Just
as Macbeth has committed an unnatural act in killing Duncan, so Henry
is about to perform a crime against Nature, but one involving birth,
rather than death.  Fritz parallels the role of the sleepy, drunken
porter as he hobbles down the stairs mumbling to himself, "Can't
have people messing about at this time of night.  Got too much to
do."  As the gate in Macbeth is metaphorically the gateway to Hell,
so the door in Frankenstein is an entry to a place where hellish
proceedings are underway.  The entrance of Victor, Elizabeth, and
Dr. Waldman contrasts the ordinary, respectable world with Henry's
unnatural one, just as Macduff and Lennox's entrance forms a contrast to the abnormal atmosphere created by Macbeth and Lady Macbeth.
The funniest episode in this scene occurs when, in a long shot, Henry
is seen stalking across his lab muttering under his breath, as if the
knocking were only interrupting a casual domestic chore, "Of all the
times for anybody to come."

When the Monster dies in the burning windmill, the movement
of the film from a break in the natural order through a period of
chaos to a restoration of order is complete.  Henry has disrupted
nature by his unnatural creation of a creature of darkness.  This
creation has resulted in chaos, sorrow, and--for Fritz, Dr. Waldman,

---

[78]Jensen, Boris Karloff, p. 34, mentions this "grotesque
variation" in passing, but does not follow up with any discussion
of the parallels.

and Maria--death. Now, order has been restored, but it is not a
very hopeful order; rather, the restoration is a pessimistic one.
This overall pattern is visualized in Henry's fall from the top of
the windmill. He falls onto one of the windmill's blades and breaks
its normal clockwise movement. For a moment, the blade moves counter-
clockwise, then dumps Henry and resumes its normal movement. Significantly, however, this normal movement is soon ended as the windmill is destroyed by flames.

Quite obviously, the film has prepared us for Henry's death.
His bond with the Monster, Elizabeth's premonition that "something
is coming between us," and Henry's instructions to Victor (who also
loves Elizabeth) before he goes to hunt the Monster, "I leave her
in your care, whatever happens, in your care," are harbingers of
Henry's death. Fortunately, the tacked-on ending is so plainly
false that it does not destroy the power of the film. As R. H. W.
Dillard states, "the last real scene in the film was at the burning
windmill, the last real shot a descent away from that windmill."[79]

---

[79]Dillard, Horror Films, p. 27. Dillard's comment on the
same page that "Orson Welles copied this shot . . . scrupulously
at the end of Citizen Kane" is open to question. Welles' final
sequence involves three dissolves, all of which move consistently
down and away from Xanadu. Whale's final sequence is a series of
six shots (only one is a dissolve), alternating shots of the windmill with shots of the Monster trapped under a fallen beam.
Welles may well have obtained his basic idea from Whale, but there
is no evidence of a "scrupulous copy." In this instance, I believe
Dillard has stretched a point in order to better accommodate his
thesis, namely, that both Frankenstein and Citizen Kane "close with
the burning of a great man's dream" (Dillard, Horror Films, p. 27).

However, even the present ending holds out little hope for
the Baron or Henry. In the last scene, Henry is seen only as a
figure in the distant background, and he and Elizabeth do not share in
the Baron's toast, "Here's to a son to the House of Frankenstein."[80]
Security, comfort, and order are no longer possible for any members
of the House of Frankenstein, for, beneath the fiery hell of the
burning windmill, the Monster waits to rise again.

Humanity fares poorly in Frankenstein. It is the key to
Whale's "dignity of [thematic] treatment"[81] that he does not shirk
from showing the bias and insensitivity of the "normal" people.
The simple villagers are easily transformed into a raging lynch mob,
more like a pack of crazed dogs than the hounds themselves; Baron
Frankenstein is an old man living in a static past; Dr. Waldman
is a good scientist, but blind to the Monster's plight; Henry is
a weak person unable to accept responsibility for his creation; and
Elizabeth and Victor are well-intentioned, but ineffective (neither
proves capable of deterring Henry from his mad dream). In The
Bride of Frankenstein, Whale's bleak view of mankind is continued
and extended.

---

[80]There was a sound practical reason for not showing any
close-ups of Henry in the ending scene: Colin Clive had already
returned to England when the scene was shot. Just before leaving,
he made the following comments: "I think Frankenstein has an intensely dramatic quality that continues throughout the play and
culminates when I am killed by the Monster I created. This is
a rather unusual ending for a talking picture, as the producers
generally prefer that the play end happily with hero and heroine
clasped in each other's arms" ("Clive of Frankenstein," New York
Times, 15 November 1931, sect. 8, p. 6).

[81]Butler, p. 50.

CHAPTER III
THE BRIDE OF FRANKENSTEIN

> It may be that I'm intended to know
> the secret of life.  It may be part
> of the Divine Plan.
>
> Henry Frankenstein

> Alone, you have created a man.  Now,
> together, we will create his mate.
>
> Dr. Pretorius (to Henry
> Frankenstein)

> Alone, bad.  Friend, good.
>
> The Monster

> Shall we put the heart in now?
>
> Henry Frankenstein (to
> Dr. Pretorius)

> We belong dead.
>
> The Monster (to Dr.
> Pretorius and the Bride)

## Background:  The Bride of Frankenstein

A sequel to Frankenstein was planned by Universal as early as

1933, but problems such as deciding upon a title and choosing a

cast delayed its making.  Originally, the title was The Return of

Frankenstein; this was shifted to Frankenstein Lives Again!, changed

to The Bride of Frankenstein, then changed back to The Return of

Frankenstein.[1]  When shooting began in January, 1935, the script

---

[1]Donald F. Glut, The Frankenstein Legend:  A Tribute to Mary
Shelley and Boris Karloff (Metuchen, N. J.:  Scarecrow Press, 1973),
pp. 121-122.

was still called The Return of Frankenstein, but when the film was released in April, 1935, the title had been finalized as The Bride of Frankenstein.[2]

The perplexity over the title was due to the studio executives' natural fear that the public would be confused as to whether "bride" referred to Henry's wife or the Monster's mate. However, by 1935, the name, Frankenstein, had become inextricably linked with the Monster in the audience's mind and there was no problem with identification.[3]

According to R. C. Sherriff, Whale was initially not eager to direct a sequel. Sherriff quotes Whale as saying in 1933,

> They're always like that. If they score a hit with a picture they always want to do it again. They've got a perfectly sound commercial reason. Frankenstein was a gold mine at the box office, and a sequel to it is bound to win, however rotten it is. They've had a script made for a sequel and it stinks to Heaven. In any case, I squeezed the idea dry on the original picture, and never want to work on it again.[4]

---

[2] Paul Jensen, Boris Karloff and His Films (New York: A. S. Barnes, 1974), p. 81.

[3] Interestingly, as early as the first film, the identification of Frankenstein with the Monster was beginning. In an interview, Karloff said, "Often when 'Frankenstein' was called--Mr. Whale would only call us by our names in the script--I would respond. Colin Clive . . . would not reply at all. Yet, of course, it should have been the other way about" (Tom Hutchinson, Horror and Fantasy in the Movies (New York: Crescent Books, 1974), p. 19).

[4] R. C. Sherriff, No Leading Lady: An Autobiography (London: Victor Gollancz, 1968), p. 269.

Whale went on to make The Invisible Man in 1933, but obviously

changed his mind about a Frankenstein sequel, proving in 1935 that he

definitely had not "squeezed the idea dry."[5]

As usual, casting proved a problem, but a minor one compared

to the difficulties encountered with Frankenstein. Colin Clive

and Boris Karloff were signed to continue their respective roles.

In 1933, Bela Lugosi had been slated to play the mad scientist,

Dr. Pretorius, but, when the film was not made at that time, he

backed out.[6] The part was given to Whale's friend from England,

Ernest Thesiger, who had appeared in The Old Dark House in 1932.

Mae Clarke was unavailable for the role of Elizabeth, and the part

was taken by young Valerie Hobson.[7] For the key role of the Bride,

---

[5] I have not been able to establish what "script" Whale is
referring to in the textual quote. Since each major studio
employed scores of writers to work on many different projects
(ranging from rough drafts to final products) at the same time,
any of the writers in the screenplay department could have done
the script. John L. Balderston, who co-authored the Frankenstein
screenplay with Garrett Fort and Francis Edward Faragoh, and
William Hurlbut ultimately received credit for Bride's script,
although many of the ideas were Whale's. Balderston later dis-
owned the film, stating that he wrote it as a satire and Laemmle,
Junior, changed it into a horror film (Denis Gifford, Karloff:
The Man, the Monster, the Movies (New York:  Curtis Books, 1973),
p. 206).

[6] Glut, The Frankenstein Legend, p. 121.  Arthur Lennig, The
Count:  The Life and Films of Bela "Dracula" Lugosi (New York:
G. P. Putnam's Sons, 1974), p. 158, states that "Universal . . .
had vague plans to star Karloff and Lugosi in it [a sequel to
Frankenstein] , but the project was postponed."

[7] Ms. Hobson (only eighteen when she made Bride) later married
John Profumo, the key figure in the sex scandal which was a major
factor in toppling Harold MacMillan's English government in 1963.

Whale selected Elsa Lanchester,[8] the wife of British actor Charles
Laughton, who had made his American film debut in The Old Dark House.
Dwight Frye returned to portray Karl, Dr. Pretorius' assistant, and
Una O'Connor was added as Minnie, a servant of the Frankensteins.
The parts of Victor and the Baron were left out entirely.

Jack Pierce again performed the make-up chores. He altered Karloff's
appearance to conform with the Monster's having been burned in the fire;
the Monster's face was scarred and scorched, and his clothing was torn
and burned. As Paul Jensen notes, this was the only time in any of
the Universal Frankenstein films[9] when the survival of the Monster
(he falls through the floor of the windmill into a flooded cellar)

---

[8]Pierce gave Ms. Lanchester a Queen Nefertiti-style hair-do,
stitched scars on her neck to show where the head had been attached,
designed shoe lifts to raise her 5'4" height, and wrapped her so
tightly in bandages that she could not move, had to be carried
around the set, and fed liquids by tube. Ms. Lanchester's wry
reaction to her situation was a typical bit of British understatement:
"It would have been easy to grow hysterical" (Denis Gifford, A
Pictorial History of Horror Movies (London: Hamlyn Publishing Group,
1973), p. 111).

[9]In addition to Frankenstein and Bride, there were six other
Universal films involving the Monster. Whale was not connected
with any of them. Karloff played the Monster once more in Son of
Frankenstein (1939), directed by Rowland V. Lee. Son of Frankenstein
is quite effective in its own right, creating a nightmare world of
constant rain and darkness, and featuring excellent performances by
Bela Lugosi as Ygor (a shepherd with a broken neck), Lionel Atwill
(a one-armed police chief), Basil Rathbone (Henry Frankenstein's son),
and, of course, Karloff. From this point, however, the films go
rapidly downhill. The Ghost of Frankenstein (1942) and Frankenstein
Meets the Wolf Man (1943) both have effective moments, but neither
comes close to matching the power of the original films, while House
of Frankenstein (1944) and House of Dracula (1945) are mindless works
with plots which defy synopsis. Universal's last entry in the series,
Abbott and Costello Meet Frankenstein (1948), was actually a well-
done spoof, paving the way for such modern parodies as Mel Brooks'
Young Frankenstein (1974).

was, at least, possible.[10] This close attention to plot detail

demonstrates the truth of R. C. Sherriff's assertion that "Whale

was a perfectionist. He would spend time on small details that

most people would have thought too trivial to worry about."[11]

The actual shooting of the film encountered difficulties

immediately when Karloff dislocated his hip in a fall and required

massage and infra-red heat treatments after each day's work.[12]

Amazingly, filming was not interrupted, although Karloff lost

twenty pounds during the thirty-two days of shooting.[13]

Originally, Bride was approximately ninety minutes long, but,

for final release, it was trimmed to about seventy-five minutes.

Most of the excised portions were from a sub-plot involving the

homicidal maniac, Karl (Dwight Frye).[14] Karl survives in the

present version as an assistant to Dr. Pretorius, but his part

has been considerably reduced.

---

[10]Jensen, Boris Karloff, p. 89.

[11]Sherriff, p. 148.

[12]Jensen, Boris Karloff, p. 89.

[13]Ibid. The filming was enlivened by such entertaining in-
cidents as the following, related by Karloff: "The watery
opening . . . was filmed with me wearing a rubber suit under my
costume to ward off chill. But air got into my suit. When I
was launched in the pond, my legs flew up in the air, and I floated
there like some sort of obscene water lily while I, and everyone
else, hooted with laughter. They finally fished me out with a
boathook and deflated me" (Boris Karloff, "Memoirs of a Monster,"
Saturday Evening Post, v. 235 (3 November 1962), p. 80).

[14]Richard Bojarski and Kenneth Beale, The Films of Boris
Karloff (Secaucus, N. J.: Citadel Press, 1974), p. 102.

As in Frankenstein, the conclusion of Bride was revised. The most gruesome (but dramatically most appropriate) ending called for Karl to kill Elizabeth and have Henry unknowingly use her heart as the animating force of the Bride.[15] This version never reached the filming stage, but one in which Henry and Elizabeth are both killed in the laboratory explosion (Elizabeth escapes from Karl's clutches and arrives at the laboratory just as it explodes) was actually shot. When it was decided that they should live, the set had been destroyed and was too expensive to rebuild, so the scene was edited to make it appear that Henry and Elizabeth escape. Universal gambled that everyone would be watching the collapsing laboratory equipment, and would not notice that Henry was present.[16] The gamble succeeded; however, in the two brief shots which remain of the laboratory's exploding interior, Henry can be clearly seen (if one looks closely) in the lower left hand portion of the screen. The studio also removed the "happy ending" from the still-circulating prints of Frankenstein, since in Bride, Henry is shown reviving after being carried home (the epilogue was restored when Frankenstein was released to television in the 1950's).

When Bride was released, the reviews were enthusiastic. The acute critic, Otis Ferguson, reviewed Bride in conjunction with John Ford's The Informer and felt that Bride was the superior

---

[15]Gifford, A Pictorial History, p. 115.

[16]Bojarski and Beale, p. 102, and Glut, The Frankenstein Legend, p. 131.

work, concluding that "a great deal of art has gone into the planning and taking of whole portions of this film."[17] Time found the movie "fully the equal of Frankenstein"[18] and the New York Times stated that "James Whale . . . has done another excellent job; the setting, photography, and make-up . . . contribute their important elements to a first-rate horror film."[19] The contemporary critics have not been the only ones impressed with Bride. Among present-day writers on film, John Baxter, Calvin Thomas Beck, John Brosnan, Carlos Clarens, Radu Florescu, Denis Gifford, Donald Glut, Charles Higham, Frank Manchel, and Ed Naha all believe Bride to be Whale's best film, and William K. Everson says Bride is "by far the best of Universal's eight Frankenstein films" and "probably also the best of the entire man-made-monster genre from any period."[20] The reasons for such widespread acclaim will now be examined.

[17]Otis Ferguson, "Two Films," New Republic, v. 73 (29 May 1935), p. 75.

[18]"The Bride of Frankenstein," Time, v. 25 (29 April 1935), p. 52.

[19]Frank S. Nugent, "The Bride of Frankenstein," New York Times, 11 May 1935, p. 21.

[20]See John Baxter, Hollywood in the Thirties (New York: Paperback Library, 1970), p. 90; John Brosnan, The Horror People (New York: St. Martin's Press, 1976), p. 50; Carlos Clarens, An Illustrated History of the Horror Film (New York: Capricorn Books, 1968), p. 68; Radu Florescu, In Search of Frankenstein (Boston: New York Graphic Society, 1975), p. 193; Gifford, Karloff, p. 55; Glut, The Frankenstein Legend, p. 132; Charles Higham, The Art of the American Film: 1900-1971 (Garden City, N. Y.: Doubleday, 1973), p. 160; Frank Manchel, Terrors of the Screen (Englewood Cliffs, N. J.: Prentice-Hall, 1970), p. 70; Ed Naha, Horrors: From Screen to Scream (New York: Avon Books, 1975), p. 27; and William K. Everson, Classics of the Horror Film (Secaucus, N. J.: Citadel Press, 1974), p. 43.

## Analysis:  The Bride of Frankenstein

In a prologue, Lord Byron (Gavin Gordon) and Percy Shelley
(Douglas Walton) convince Mary Shelley (Elsa Lanchester) to
continue her story of Frankenstein.  The scene shifts to the
burning windmill where Maria's father (nameless in Frankenstein),
Hans (Reginald Barlow), and his wife (Mary Gordon) stand watching
the smoldering ruins.  Hans falls through the floor and is strangled
by the Monster (Boris Karloff), who has survived by falling into
the flooded cellar.  The Monster climbs out and throws Hans'
wife into the cellar.  Back at the Frankenstein home, Henry (Colin
Clive) is found to be alive.  While recuperating, he receives a
visit from his old professor, Dr. Pretorius (Ernest Thesiger),
who tells Henry of his own experiments in creating life.  Intrigued,
Henry goes with Pretorius to his lodgings, where Pretorius pro-
duces his collection of six small homunculi and asks Henry to
collaborate with him in constructing a "mate" for the Monster.
Meanwhile, the Monster rescues a shepherdess (Ann Darling) from
drowning, but is set upon by the villagers, captured, and im-
prisoned.  He breaks free and terrorizes the village.  Wandering
through the countryside, he is befriended by a blind hermit (O.
P. Heggie), but this idyll is interrupted by two hunters who
attack the Monster and drive him away, destroying the hermit's
hut in the process.  The Monster staggers into a cemetery, enters
an  underground crypt, and encounters Pretorius, who is robbing
graves.  Pretorius decides the Monster can be of use to him in
dealing with Henry.  Next, Pretorius goes to the Frankenstein

mansion and, when Henry informs him that he has changed his mind about their collaboration, he orders the Monster to kidnap Elizabeth (Valerie Hobson) in order to ensure Henry's cooperation. Pretorius' assistant, Karl (Dwight Frye), murders a young girl to obtain the needed fresh heart and, in a spectacular scene, Henry and Pretorius create a Bride (Elsa Lanchester) for the Monster, but she rejects him. The grief-stricken Monster destroys the labotatory, killing himself, the Bride, and Pretorius, but he allows Henry and Elizabeth to escape.

The prologue, while not part of the main thrust of the film, is an interesting display of Whale's talents. First, on the plot level, it functions nicely to review Frankenstein (scenes from the earlier film are intercut with Byron's description of them). Second, the crashing thunder and flashing lightning set an ominous tone for the remainder of the film. Third, Whale uses the opening to subtly satirize Byron, Shelley, and, by extension, the Romantic movement; the high-key lighting and the gliding camera movements serve to emphasize what Whale sees as the surface gloss and super-ficiality of Byron and Shelley. Fourth, and most important, the sequence stresses Mary Shelley's link with her literary creation. By using the same actress to play both Mary Shelley and the Bride, Whale indicates his belief that "Mary Shelley had something in common with the dreadful creature of her imagination. . . . James Whale felt that frustration and wrath in a woman often lay under an excess of sweetness and light."[21]

---

[21]Elsa Lanchester, "Letter to the Editor," Life, v. 64 (5 April 1968), p. 21.

From the nineteenth century prologue, the film suddenly jumps
forward almost one hundred years.[22] We are back at the burning
windmill and the Monster's first appearance is a chilling one. Hans,
Maria's father, falls into the flooded cellar. At first, only the
Monster's right hand can be seen behind a beam, then his scarred,
burned, hate-filled face slowly emerges. He moves swiftly forward
and strangles Hans. The Monster then rises from the watery cellar
and extends his hand through the floor opening. Hans' wife, thinking
it is her husband, grasps his hand and pulls him up. The Monster
responds by throwing her through the opening. Immediately, we know
that this is a very different, very dangerous Monster, one no longer
ignorant or innocent.[23] Whale artfully conveys this fact by intercutting

---

[22]The time of the Frankenstein films has been a source of
confusion. The clothing appears roughly contemporary, but the
settings seem nineteenth century. There are no automobiles, only
carriages. In Dr. Pretorius' grave-robbing scene, the date on a
casket is 1899. In Frankenstein, a hanged man is cut down from
a public gibbet, and, according to Glut, The Frankenstein Legend,
p. 147, the practice of leaving hanged men on display had been abandoned in Europe before 1900. In Bride, Henry talks with Elizabeth
on a telephone (called an "electrical machine" in the film). Glut,
The Frankenstein Legend, p. 147, says that the telephone was
patented in 1876 (of course, this means little; a scientist of
Pretorius' ability would certainly be capable of besting Alexander
Graham Bell). Far from detracting from the films, I feel this
ambiguity involving time contributes to the mysterious, mythic,
"time-lessness" of the legend.

[23]In an interview, Karloff emphasized that both he and
Whale thought of the Monster as originally innocent: "Whale and
I both saw the character as an innocent one. . . . I tried to
play it that way. This was a pathetic creature who . . . had
neither wish nor say in his creation. . . . The most heart-
rending aspect of the creature's life, for us, was his ultimate
desertion by his creator. It was as though man, in his blundering,
searching attempts to improve himself, was to find himself deserted
by his God" (Gifford, Karloff, p. 45).

shots of an owl watching the murders. The owl is a bird of prey
(loss of innocence) and is traditionally associated with wisdom
(loss of ignorance); it is also a nocturnal animal, and  thus  reinforces the darkness motif.[24]  Significantly, Hans and his wife are
the first persons the Monster has cold-bloodedly slain.  His other
killings were motivated by fear (Fritz) and self-preservation (Dr.
Waldman), or were accidental (Maria), but this "new" Monster seethes
with hate for mankind.

As the Monster wanders away down the hillside from the windmill, he exemplifies one of the main structuring patterns of Bride--
its use of vertical (up and down) movement. (R. H. W. Dillard discusses this pattern exhaustively in reference to Frankenstein, but
he does not mention Bride.)[25]       From the burning windmill,
Henry is carried down to his home.  The Monster rises up from the
water, then throws Hans' wife down into the cellar.  The shepherdess falls
from a ledge down into the pond, and is rescued by the Monster who  lifts
her up out of the water.  The Monster is chased up a hill where he
is captured by the villagers, hoisted up onto a pole, and dumped
down into a cart.  He is then taken down into a dungeon-like jail,
but he escapes and goes up into the street.  He finds temporary

---

[24] In medieval Europe, owls were considered omens of ill
fortune and were often crucified alive on barn doors (Cards of
Knowledge (Lausanne, Switzerland:  Editions Rencontre, 1976),
s.v. "Little Owl").  This fact buttresses the religious symbolism of later
scenes, in which Whale plainly intends to identify the Monster with
Christ.

[25] R. H. W. Dillard, Horror Films (New York:  Monarch Press,
1976), pp. 28-31.

sanctuary when he goes down into the crypt and, when he kidnaps
Elizabeth, he carries her up to a mountain cave. The Bride is
created by being raised up into the sky on a glittering (obviously
phallic) electrical device (as the device is raised, Karl cries out
with sexual suggestiveness, "It's coming up!") and then lowered
back down into the laboratory.

The vertical pattern is also used for humor. For example,
Pretorius' tiny king climbs up out of his jar, is picked up with
tweezers, and put back down into the jar.[26] When Pretorius brings
the Monster to see Henry, the Monster reverses the line from Frankenstein and tells Henry, "Sit down!"

As with Frankenstein, the general movement of Bride is downward, and, also as in Frankenstein, upward movements are concluded
by downward ones. Thus, in the cataclysmic ending, the Monster
blows up the tower and it collapses in a final spectacular downward movement of destruction. Also crashing down is Pretorius'
insane dream of creating a master race.

The vertical movement of Frankenstein and Bride is not solely
a structuring pattern, but also a metaphor for the height of Henry's
aspiration, his desire to do something no one else has ever done--
create life. And, since the upward movements are followed by downward ones, the entire pattern forms a prolepsis of Henry's future.

The up and down structure is not the only resemblance between
Frankenstein and Bride. For instance, the use of paired characters

-------

[26]This is an "in joke." The king is dressed exactly like
Charles Laughton (Elsa Lanchester's husband) in his Oscar-winning
role of Henry VIII.

occurs also in <u>Bride</u>. Thus, Pretorius may be seen as the dark side of Henry's nature. It becomes obvious early in the film that Henry is basically unchanged and, therefore, susceptible to the lures of his baser instincts (i.e., Pretorius). Elizabeth begs him to forget the past, and he replies,

<u>Henry</u>:  Forget! If only I could forget, but it's never out of my mind. I've been cursed for delving into the mysteries of life. Perhaps death is sacred and I've profaned it. (<u>Suddenly his face lights up</u>) Oh, what a wonderful vision it was. I dreamed of being the first to give to the world the secret which God is so jealous of--the formula for life. Think of the power to create a man. And I did it. I created a man and, who knows, in time I could have trained him to do my will. I could have bred a race. I might even have found the secret of eternal life.

<u>Elizabeth</u>:  Henry, don't say those things, don't think them. It's blasphemous and wicked. We are not meant to know those things.

<u>Henry</u>:  It may be that I'm intended to know the secret of life. It may be part of the Divine Plan.

Given this situation, Pretorius has little trouble convincing Henry to join in creating a mate for the Monster. Henry tries to subdue his dark side, forcing Pretorius to kidnap Elizabeth, but, once caught up in the frenzy of the creation, Henry is as eager as ever. During the creation scene, Whale unites Henry and Pretorius by a series of tilted angle shots; a shot of Pretorius leaning right will be followed by a shot of Henry leaning left to form a group of reverse or "mirror" images. The same feverish excitement appears on both faces.

Of course, Henry and the Monster continue to be linked. Even the Monster, in his new-found wisdom, is aware of this bond. When Pretorius asks him if he knows who Henry Frankenstein is, the

Monster replies, "Yes. Made me from dead." The clearest indication
that Henry and the Monster are united comes when the Monster is sent
by Pretorius to abduct Elizabeth. As the Monster opens the door,
Elizabeth says, "Is that you, Henry?"; Whale then cuts to a shot of
the Monster entering from behind Elizabeth. Thus, when Elizabeth
calls for her husband, she is answered by his creation, emphasizing
the ineradicable tie between creator and creation.

Another motif carried over from Frankenstein is Whale's use
of hands. The first view we have of the Monster focuses on his
hand, and his hand is immediately seen again in close-up as he
reaches up from the cellar to grasp Hans' wife. The first sign
that Henry is alive comes when Minnie sees his hand move. In
a macabre touch, a dismembered hand hangs from the ceiling in
Pretorius' laboratory. Hands are also very important in the
Monster's meeting with the hermit (this scene will be analyzed
in detail below) and in the creation scene. In the creation
sequence, Whale employs repeated close-ups of hands to bring
together all the threads of the plot, emphasize the creative-
destructive dichotomy, and stress Bride's link with Frankenstein.
Thus, the hands of Henry and Pretorius, as the creators, are
emphasized time after time; the hand of the Bride is highlighted
as she "comes to life"; the hands of the Monster are emphasized as he attempts to woo and caress his mate; and the Monster's
hand is seen in close-up as he pulls the lever which destroys
the tower. As Roy Huss notes, the repeated close-ups of hands

"function both as synecdoches (the part standing for the whole)
and as litotes (dramatic understatement)."[27]

A most important theme in Bride (and another echo of Frankenstein)
is Whale's use of religious symbolism. The Monster's rise
out of the flooded cellar from his supposed tomb becomes a second
perverse Resurrection for him, one destined to be much more destructive than the first. However, the most specific religious imagery
occurs when the Monster is captured by the villagers. Cornered on
top of a small hill, he is tied to a pole and hoisted aloft in a
"scene reminiscent of a Breughel Golgotha."[28] As he hangs in the
air (Whale emphasizes his agony by cutting to closer and closer shots),
his form closely resembling Christ on the cross, his captors revile
him and pelt him with sticks and stones. He is then toppled into
a cart as a peasant jabs him with a pitchfork. Taken to the jail
and chained to a huge chair (in a nice contrast, the chair is a
throne-like affair, more suited for kings than prisoners), his hands
are immobilized by metal rings. The rings are pounded into the
wood like nails and Whale cuts from a close-up of the rings to a close-
up of the Monster's grimacing, pain-wracked face. This comparison
of the Monster to Christ is both blatant and quite deliberate.

After the Monster escapes, he wanders into an Expressionist
cemetery filled with tilted crosses, slanted tombstones, and leaning

[27] Roy Huss, "Almost Eve: The Creation Scene in The Bride of
Frankenstein," in Focus on the Horror Film, eds. Roy Huss and T. J.
Ross (Englewood Cliffs, N. J.: Prentice-Hall, 1972), p. 78. Huss'
article is an excellent analysis and is highly recommended.

[28] Harvey Greenberg, The Movies on Your Mind (New York: Saturday
Review Press, 1975), p. 215.

statues. In a rage of pain and fear, he pushes over a statue of
some religious figure (it appears to be a bishop or a cardinal) and
seeks refuge in a crypt. As he descends, a statue of the Crucifixion
looms in the background. Just before he vanishes from view, the
Monster turns his body so that he is facing the same direction as
the statue, and stretches out his arms to balance himself on the
sides of the tomb; in this posture, his figure exactly copies the
Crucifixion statue. In the underground tomb, the Monster finds a
brief respite. As Martin Tropp observes, he is indeed a reverse
Christ, for "rather than Harrowing Hell, the Monster finds a home in
the world of the dead."[29]

In Bride, character development is more significant than in
Frankenstein. The Monster's evolving awareness has already been demonstrated in the opening scene. Also important to the Monster's growing
self-knowledge is the pastoral scene, the movie's most brightly-
lit sequence (the rest of the film is shot in a kind of twilight
gray resembling a Gustave Doré engraving). In this scene, the
Monster wanders through a sunlit wood. Flowers are in bloom, the
trees have leafy branches, and the chirping of birds is heard.
There is a small stream, a waterfall, and a shepherdess tending
her flock. Whale cuts from close-ups of the lambs to close-ups

---

[29]Martin Tropp, Mary Shelley's Monster: The Story of Frankenstein (Boston: Houghton Mifflin, 1976), p. 101. The Monster's
identification with the dead is bolstered by the fact that he
gains physical strength underground. When he is carried to the
subterranean prison, he offers only token resistance. But, once
underground, he suddenly acquires renewed vigor, breaks his bonds,
tears the door off its hinges, and rampages through the village.

of the Monster to show that he, too, is--or, at least, could
become--a "lamb of God." As the Monster goes to the stream to
drink, he sees his face reflected in the water. He hesitates
a moment, then smashes the reflection, vaguely perceiving that
this face makes him a hated pariah. Suddenly, the shepherdess
loses her balance and falls from a ledge into the stream. Instantly,
the Monster evidences his increased knowledge and awareness by
plunging in and rescuing her. When he threw Maria into the water,
he did not realize its destructive potential; now, he does. By
rescuing the shepherdess, he exactly reverses (and atones for)
his action with Maria, indicating that, although he is no longer
completely innocent, he could be redeemed by human kindness and
love. But this possibility is promptly dissipated by the revival
of the shepherdess, who screams in terror upon seeing the Monster's
face. Two hunters enter and shoot the Monster. Wounded in the arm,
he stumbles through a barren, surrealistic landscape, pursued by
the villagers. There are no flowers, the trees are branchless,
and the only sound is the baying of dogs and the yells of the
peasants as they engage in the "pagan sport of a mountain man-
hunt."[30] The starkness and bareness of the countryside stress the
isolation and alienation of the Monster, as well as forming an
effective counterpoint to the preceding pastoral scene.

---

[30] "James Whale and Frankenstein," New York Times, 20 December
1931, sect. 8, p. 4. Whale made this statement in regard to
Frankenstein, but it seems even more applicable to Bride.

After escaping from his underground incarceration, the Monster encounters the blind hermit in a sequence which has been described as "one of the most sensitive and curious in the monster cinema."[31] A shot analysis of this scene follows:

Setting: The hermit's hut.

Shot No.

1-2.    Medium shot of the hermit playing "Ave Maria" on his violin (1), followed by a close-up of the Monster outside looking through the window (2). He is obviously moved by the music.

Cut to:
3.    Close-up of the hermit. His hands are highlighted.

Comment: This shot is a good example of Whale's use of lighting and camera placement to make his point. The scene is lit so that the hands are brighter than anything else in the frame, and the camera is placed so that they are near the center of the frame; thus, the shot emphasizes and prominently features the hands.

Cut to:
4-9.    Alternating medium shots of the Monster and the hermit. During the sequence, the Monster throws open the door and enters the hut.

Cut to:
10.    Medium shot of the hermit.

Hermit: "Who are you? I think you're a stranger to me. I cannot see you. I cannot see anything."

The hermit moves toward the door.

Cut to:
11.    A slightly closer medium shot of the hermit.

Hermit: "You must please excuse me, but I'm blind."

---

[31]Chris Steinbrunner and Burt Goldblatt, Cinema of the Fantastic (New York: Saturday Review Press, 1972), p. 101.

Comment: The use of a shot followed by a slightly closer
shot (as in shots 10 and 11), or one from a
slightly different angle, is a favorite technique of Whale's. He uses it to upset audience
expectations, to keep them from relaxing and,
thereby, dissipating the tension.[32]

Cut to:
12-16. Alternating close-ups of the Monster and the
hermit.

Hermit: "Come in, my poor friend. None will hurt
you here. If you're in trouble, perhaps
I can help you. But you don't need to
tell me about it if you don't want to."

Comment: In this sequence, Karloff artfully portrays the
Monster's feelings. He is obviously touched, but
also seems puzzled. It is literally the first time
that any adult has displayed kindness to him. Unsure
how to react, his bewilderment shows.

Cut to:
17-19. Slightly varied medium shots of the Monster and the
hermit. The hermit leads the Monster into the house.
As the hermit pulls the Monster into the room, his
hands are highlighted as in shot 3. In shot 19, the
hermit guides the Monster to a chair.

Hermit: "Sit down."

The Monster obeys and the hermit places both hands
on the Monster's shoulders.

Hermit: "I don't understand. Can you not speak?
It's strange. Perhaps you're afflicted, too.
I cannot see and you cannot speak. Is that
it? If you understand what I'm saying, put
your hand on my shoulder."

---

[32]This is a variation of G. W. Pabst's "cutting on movement."
Pabst discovered that, if a cut were made during an act of motion
(the movement of an arm or leg, the opening of a door, etc.), the
cut would usually go unnoticed by the audience. For a discussion
of Pabst's concept and its implications, see any good film history
text, such as Arthur Knight, The Liveliest Art: A Panoramic History
of the Movies, revised edition (New York: Macmillan Publishing Co.,
1978), pp. 51-55.

The Monster lifts his right hand and drops it heavily on the hermit's left shoulder.

Hermit: "That's good."

Comment: For the first time, the Monster hears the words, "Sit down," spoken in a gentle tone. In the hermit's hut, the command and the downward movement do not have  negative connotations.

Cut to:
20.    Medium shot of the hermit and the Monster from behind the Monster. He tries to rise.

Hermit: "No, you stay here. I'll get you some food."

The hermit moves to a kettle hanging over the fire in the background and begins to ladle out soup into a bowl.

Hermit: "We shall be friends."

Comment: This shot is an excellent example of Whale's understanding of when not to cut. For the maximum emotional effect of the scene, it is important that both the Monster and the hermit be in the frame when the hermit declares that they shall be "friends."

Cut to:
21-23.  Two medium shots of the hermit giving soup to the Monster (21-22), followed by a close-up of the hermit (23). In shot 21, a crucifix on the wall is visible for the first time.

Hermit: "I have prayed many times for God to send me a friend. It's very lonely here and its been a long time since any human being came into this hut."

Comment: The pathetic  ironies of this speech cannot be missed. The creature whom the hermit is depending upon to ease his loneliness is not a "human being" at all. Indeed, when human beings eventually enter the hut, the idyll will be destroyed.

Cut to:
24-27.  Medium shots of the hermit and the Monster, as the Monster hungrily drinks the soup.

Hermit: "I shall look after you and you will comfort me. Now you must lie down and go to sleep."

Cut to:
28-35.  A series of close-ups of the Monster and the hermit,
combined with medium shots which include both
characters. The "Ave Maria" is heard on the soundtrack as the hermit prays.

> Hermit:  "Our Father, we thank Thee that in Thy
> great mercy, Thou hast taken pity on my
> great loneliness and now out of the silence
> of the night hast brought two of Thy lonely
> children together and sent me a friend to
> be a light to mine eyes and a comfort in
> time of trouble. Amen."

In shot 35, the crucifix in the background suddenly
lights up. The remainder of the scene fades, leaving
the illuminated crucifix (in the top center portion
of the screen) shining.

Comment:  The "Ave Maria" and the hermit's prayer are, in the
context, supremely ironic. It is obvious that these
two "lonely children" will not be able to share
happiness in this world due to man's interference.
In shot 34, a single tear rolls down the Monster's
cheek. This tear will be matched by another which
is shed just prior to the Monster's destruction of
the laboratory. Now it is a tear of joy, then it
will be a tear of sorrow.
    The last eight shots (28-35) are perfectly
balanced by Whale. There are two close-ups of the
Monster (31, 34), two close-ups of the hermit (29,
32), two low angle medium shots (28, 33), and two
high angle medium shots (30, 35). This rhythmic
balance helps the sequence achieve its maximum
emotional impact of touching warmth. As Michael
Gould says, "the blind fiddler, who shows the
Monster goodness, imbues his scene with such
emotional truth that the crucifix in the cottage
lights up with a sympathetic vibration."[33]

This touching scene is followed by a serio-comic one in which

the hermit teaches the Monster to talk. In a sequence with obvious

religious overtones, the hermit, dressed in what appears to be a

monk's robe, gives the Monster a "Last Supper" of bread and wine.

---

[33]Michael Gould, Surrealism and the Cinema (New York: A. S.
Barnes, 1976), p. 55.

He teaches the Monster that "bread" is "good," "wine" is "good,"
"alone" is "bad," and, most importantly, that "friend" is "good."
He also gives the Monster a cigar and, in an amusing touch, plays
a rollicking tune on his violin while the Monster smokes and keeps
time to the music with his hands and feet. But, just at this
moment, the outside world intrudes in the form of two hunters who
are lost in the woods. Seeing the Monster, they attack him; in
the ensuing struggle, a bundle of reeds is knocked into the fireplace and the Monster is driven from the cottage by his old
nemesis, fire. As he staggers out the door, he cries in a
pathetic voice, "Friend? Friend?"

The entire Monster-hermit episode is filled with ironies.
As noted above, the Monster is still capable of being redeemed by
love and human decency. The hermit is the perfect choice to be the
instrument of this redemption since he is innocent and pure, and,
although blind, is the only human who "sees" beneath the surface
to the innate goodness within the Monster. However, it quickly
becomes obvious that there is no possibility of the Monster being
redeemed or leading a happy life. The only "friend" he has found
is an afflicted outcast like himself, and society does not tolerate
such outcasts for long. As long as the Monster and the hermit are
isolated in the hut, their happiness is assured, but their haven
is a frail defense against the outside world and, as soon as
representatives of that world enter, their peaceful existence is
destroyed, just as the hut itself is demolished by fire.

From his meeting with the hermit, the Monster gains not only a knowledge of speech, but also a darker knowledge; namely, that humanity despises him because, through no fault of his own, he "disturbs the balance of respectable society by looking like and being a monster."[34]

Karloff was opposed to having the Monster speak,[35] yet surely this is a logical character development as his newly-awakened mind matures. As Paul Jensen notes, the Monster's "hesitancy of action and dimness of mind [in Frankenstein] are replaced [in Bride] with awkwardness and awareness."[36] The Monster's growing maturity culminates in the creation scene when he, not the humans, asserts the proper moral priorities by telling Pretorius, "We belong dead," and then destroys the tower, implicitly recognizing that "there can be no place in the land of the living for creatures of death."[37]

In contrast to the Monster, Henry Frankenstein gains no self-knowledge during the course of the film. In his first scene, he reminisces about "what a wonderful vision it [the creation of life]

---

[34]Stanley Solomon, Beyond Formula: American Film Genres (New York: Harcourt Brace Jovanovich, 1976), p. 134.

[35]Karloff explained his reasoning in the following manner: "Speech! Stupid! My argument was that if the monster had any impact or charm, it was because he was inarticulate--this great, lumbering, inarticulate creature. The moment he spoke, you might as well take the mick or play it straight" (Brosnan, The Horror People, p. 50). Considering his opposition to Whale's interpretation of the role, Karloff's impeccable performance is even more amazing.

[36]Jensen, Boris Karloff, p. 36.

[37]Tropp, p. 104.

was," and in his other scenes, he appears as a weak, vacillating man. In his first conversation with Pretorius, Henry tells him, "I'll have no more of this Hell-spawn," but quickly changes his mind when Pretorius informs him that he, too, has created life. Henry eagerly asks, "When can I see it?" and despite his initial protestations, agrees to help Pretorius create a mate for the Monster.[38] Under Elizabeth's influence, Henry changes his mind again and refuses to cooperate. However, in the creation scene, Henry shows as much zeal as Pretorius. As Roy Huss has shown in his previously mentioned essay, Whale handles this scene with great skill, using shots of Henry and Pretorius racing back and forth across the laboratory to convey an air of freneticism, and tilted camera angles to stress the "tilted," unbalanced minds of the scientists and the distorted nature of the experiment. As the frenzied activity reaches a peak, Henry shows his total commitment to the project by saying eagerly to Pretorius, "Shall we put the heart in now?"[39] Ironically, at the end, Henry is saved from the consequences of his folly by the Monster, who tells him, "You go, you live."[40]

---

[38]Jensen, Boris Karloff, p. 82, states that it is "odd" that Pretorius should propose creating a mate before he knows the Monster is alive, but this is Jensen's error. In the first conversation between Pretorius and Henry, Pretorius plainly makes reference to "your Monster still roaming the countryside" before he suggests creating a woman.

[39]Oddly, Huss, p. 78, attributes this important line mistakenly to Pretorius.

[40]However, this irony is surely unintended since Whale wanted Henry to die in the explosion also. Certainly, the Monster has as much reason to hate Henry as Pretorius.

Elsa Lanchester as the Bride has a small (although important) part, which she imbues with "dramatic sparks as though through her frizzed-out hair."[41] The introduction of the Bride is a variation of the Monster's introduction, and may be described as follows:

Setting: Henry's laboratory, just after the successful creation of the Bride.

Shot No.

1. Medium long shot of the Bride with Henry on her right and Pretorius on her left. The Bride wears a long white gown draped over her bandages.

Comment: The Bride is flanked by her symbolic parents, "as if posing for an official wedding photograph."[42] The long, loose-flowing gown is a perfect choice of apparel because it simultaneously suggests a wedding dress, a laboratory smock, and a shroud.

Quick cut to:
2. Medium shot of the Bride from straight ahead. Her hair protrudes straight up in a parody of Nefertiti.

Comment: The use of the Nefertiti hair-do is not simply a visual device. Nefertiti and her husband, Ikhnaton, are thought by some scholars to have been brother and sister.[43] Similarly, the Monster and his mate are both "children" of Henry Frankenstein, and, thus, siblings.

Quick cut to:
3. Medium close shot of the Bride.

Quick cut to:
4. Low angle close-up of the Bride. The stitches in her neck are emphasized. She turns her head jerkily to look left, then right, then up.

---

[41]Hutchinson, p. 42.

[42]Huss, p. 82.

[43]Encyclopedia Brittanica, 1969 ed., s.v. "Ikhnaton," by Margaret Stefano Drower.

Pretorius announces grandly, "the Bride of Frankenstein," to the accompaniment of wedding bells on the sound track. The Monster enters and gestures to the Bride, but, terrified of him, she shrieks and runs to her "father," Henry. Henry leads her to the Monster, who touchingly tries to woo her by stroking her hand, but she screams again and retreats. The Monster, recognizing his total isolation, says, "She hate me, like others," and destroys the laboratory. If one looks closely at the destruction scene, the Bride may be seen running to, rather than from, the Monster, as the tower collapses. Thus, although she refuses the mate selected for her, she joins him in death. Hence, in a supreme irony, the two monsters, not man, make the correct moral choices, the Bride by rejecting the future planned for her, and the Monster by recognizing that they "belong dead."

The most interesting character in Bride is Dr. Pretorius. His name is obviously important since, in his initial appearance, Minnie repeats it four times, Henry says it twice, and Pretorius himself states it twice. Pretorius combines the Latin for leader (praetor) with that for law (iūs). He wants to be a dictator whose word is law. In this desire, he is "a perfect parody of a would-be Hitler"[44] who will stop at nothing to obtain his ends. To gain these ends, Pretorius uses Henry to help him create life and, when Henry refuses to cooperate, uses the Monster to kidnap Elizabeth. He pretends to

---

[44]Tropp, p. 104.

be the Monster's friend but, when the Monster appears to be
impeding progress, he callously drugs his drink. Pretorius intends
to use the Monster and the Bride to produce a master race. In his
toast, "To a new world of gods and monsters," Pretorius sees himself as a god who will control a race of monsters.

Martin Tropp has pointed out how Pretorius, with his black
costume and medieval skull-cap, is similar to a "new alchemist."[45]
He also resembles a priest, but a priest of the dead, not of the
living, and he is explicitly identified with death on several
occasions. Just before Pretorius' first entrance, Elizabeth tells
Henry that she feels a "strange apparition" coming toward them and
then cries, "It comes, a figure like Death"; immediately there
comes a knock at the door and Pretorius enters. When Henry first
enters Pretorius' laboratory, he shivers as if from the coldness
of the grave. The laboratory contains a severed hand hanging from
the ceiling, and skeletons and skulls in the background. Pretorius
keeps his tiny homunculi in a casket-shaped box and he says of the
underground crypt, "I rather like this place." He dines on a
coffin with a skull and human bones for table ornaments. When the
Monster says that he hates the living and loves the dead, Pretorius
comments, "You're wise in your choice."

Another of Pretorius' functions is to serve as an outlet for
Whale's satiric thrusts at religion.       He tells Henry that

---

[45]Ibid., p. 99.

"I, also, have created life, as we say, in God's own image," and
"Leave the charnel house and follow the lead of Nature, or of God,
if you like your Bible stories." In comparing himself to his
miniature devil, Pretorius says, "I have often wondered if life
wouldn't be much more amusing if we were all devils, and no non-
sense about angels and being good."

Pretorius also supplies much of the outré humor in the film.
When he first arrives at Henry's home, he announces that he has
come "on a secret matter of grave importance." In his toast, "To
a new world of gods and monsters," he drinks gin from a laboratory
beaker. Preparatory to showing Henry his homunculi, Pretorius
comments, "Science, like love, has her little surprises." His
homunculi are bizarre jokes in themselves, but Pretorius' comments
are even more humorous.          In describing his king, queen, and
archbishop, he says, "My first experiment was so lovely we made
her a queen. Then, we had to have a king, and now they're so
madly in love, I have to keep them separate. This little fellow
was so disapproving of the other two that I made him an archbishop."
Of his ballerina, Pretorius says, "My little ballerina is charming,
but such a bore. She won't dance to anything but Mendelssohn's
'Spring Song' and it gets so monotonous." Regarding the devil, he
states, "There's a certain resemblance to me, don't you think? Or
do I flatter myself?" Speaking of his mermaid, Pretorius notes that
she is the result of "an experiment with seaweed" which went awry.
Pretorius' most outrageous moments occur when he is cheerfully
grave-robbing. Using a coffin as a table, he dines on chicken and

wine. Abruptly, the Monster appears. Without batting an eyelash, Pretorius remarks, "Oh, I thought I was alone," and calmly offers the Monster a smoke, "Have a cigar. They're my only weakness."[46]

These actions are a good example of Paul Jensen's perceptive statement that "while Henry is a normal man whose nervousness makes him appear insane, Pretorius is mad, but he does outrageous things as though they were everyday occurrences "[47] (Jensen's emphasis).

Strengthening the artistry of Bride is Whale's skillful use of Franz Waxman's musical score. In the homunculi scene, we hear royal, coronation-type music as Pretorius presents his king and queen; religious organ music for the archbishop; Meldelssohn's "Spring Song" for the ballerina; a lilting, "devilish" tune for the devil; and a "siren song" for the mermaid. When the villagers gather their torches for another monster hunt, a victory march is

---

[46]Pretorius has earlier used this line when offering Henry a drink. "Do you like gin? It's my only weakness." The "gin" remark is an echo from The Old Dark House when the Thesiger character, Horace Femm, makes the same statement, proof that Whale definitely worked on the dialogue of his films.

[47]Jensen, Boris Karloff, p. 87. That Whale saw Henry as a highly-strung person, but not mad, is established by a letter from him to Clive before the filming of Frankenstein began. "I see Frankenstein as an intensely sane person, at times rather fanatical, and in one or two scenes a little hysterical. . . . Frankenstein's nerves are all to pieces. He is a very strong, extremely dominant personality, sometimes quite strange and queer, sometimes very soft and decidedly romantic. . . . He is pulled two ways--his love for Elizabeth and his almost insane passion for his experiments. . . . All the time, one should feel that Frankenstein is normally and extremely intelligent, a sane . . . person" ("Clive of Frankenstein," New York Times, 15 November 1931, sect. 8, p. 6).

heard. As the Monster wanders through the pastoral landscape, the melody is soft, low, and soothing (except for one discordant note when the Monster sees his reflection), but when he is pursued by the townspeople, the sound is loud and harsh. Waxman's score is most effective in the creation scene. Rather surprisingly, Paul Jensen misses the entire point of this sequence. Jensen states that the creation scene in Bride is superior to the one in Frankenstein "except that just as the body is raised to the roof of the laboratory, and the tension should be building to its climax, the background music shifts into a quiet, almost romantic melody that short-circuits the emotional effect."[48] This "short-circuiting" effect is exactly what Whale intends. The viewer is expecting the music to build to a climax and Whale neatly thwarts this expectation. In so doing, he sustains the ironic, sarcastic viewpoint which has been used throughout the film. Whale reinforces his satiric point by the use of wedding bells when the Bride is introduced. Although Jensen sees this touch as "pure indulgence," it is very effective and entirely consistent in tone with the rest of the film. [49]

Once again, the overall plot pattern of a break in nature, a pattern of chaos, and a return to order is maintained. In Bride,

---

[48] Jensen, Boris Karloff, p. 84.

[49] Ibid., p. 85. However, I agree with Jensen's criticism of Una O'Connor's "low grade farce" (p. 85). This broad humor does not mesh well with Whale's sophisticated graveside wit. Ms. O'Connor's scenes in The Invisible Man work somewhat better, but even there, they grow tiresome.

the breech has actually occurred before the film begins, since the
Monster still lives, but the film moves inexorably toward a second
major disruption of the natural process, the creation of another
monster. Order is restored when the Monster destroys himself, the
Bride, and Pretorius, but little hope results from this new order.
Henry is still alive and we have seen how easily swayed he is,
and, more importantly, we have seen the prejudice, ignorance, and
callousness of man prominently displayed.

Humanity fares as poorly in Bride as in Frankenstein. The
ignorant villagers are easily changed into a bloodthirsty mob;
Henry continues to be changeable and weak, still refusing to
accept proper responsibility for his creation, yet unable to
resist the excitement of another abnormal act; Elizabeth is once
more well-intentioned, but ineffective; the Burgomaster is a vain,
arrogant politician; Karl is a homicidal maniac; and Pretorius is
literally a madman who casually crushes anyone in his way. The
blind hermit remains the one truly "good" man, but his frail
physique and physical handicap cannot withstand the viciousness
of the outside world. Whale is not totally unsympathetic to his
human characters, but he does see mankind as having certain basic
flaws which inevitably surface. He always makes us feel that the
Monster could possibly lead an ordinary life, but due to man's
bigotry and narrow-mindedness, he will never get such a chance.

As T. J. Ross states, the "ultimate point of outrage" is the "denial to a creature made in the image of man of either home or homemaking Eve."[50]

In an interview with Tom Hutchinson, Boris Karloff stated,

> I don't think Bob Florey really intended there to be much pathos inside the character [the Monster]. But Whale and I thought that there should be. . . . Otherwise our audience just wouldn't think about the film after they'd left the theatre and Whale very much wanted them to do that. He wanted to make some impact on them.[51]

The impact which Whale made was bleak and despairing, but profoundly artistic.

---

[50]T. J. Ross, "Introduction," in Focus on the Horror Film, p. 3.

[51]Hutchinson, p. 132.

CHAPTER IV
THE INVISIBLE MAN

He's invisible, that's what's the
matter with him.

Constable Jaffers

Suddenly I realized the power I
held, the power to rule, to make
the world grovel at my feet.

Jack Griffin (to Dr. Kemp)

I meddled in things which man must
leave alone.

Jack Griffin (to Flora)

Background:  The Invisible Man

Universal first considered The Invisible Man as a vehicle for

Boris Karloff in 1931, but the technical knowledge needed to produce

the special effects was not yet available.  Attempts to manipulate

articles of clothing by wires did not give the look of a full-bodied

man and efforts to use mirrors were also unsuccessful.[1]

---

[1]Jeff Rovin, Movie Special Effects (New York:  A. S. Barnes,
1977), p. 47.  Both Donald Glut, Classic Movie Monsters (Metuchen,
N. J.:  Scarecrow Press, 1978), p. 132, and Paul Jensen, "The
Invisible Man:  A Retrospective," Photon, no. 23 (1973), p. 10,
state that Robert Florey was originally scheduled to direct, but
Florey himself is silent on the matter.  Stephen Pendo, "Universal's
Golden Age of Horror:  1931-1941," Films in Review, v. 26 (March
1975), p. 157, says that Florey, Cyril Gardner, and E. A. Dupont
all came and went before Whale took over.
     In 1931, Universal bought the rights to a Philip Wylie novel,
The Murderer Invisible (New York:  Holt, Rinehart and Winston, 1931;
paperback reprint edition, New York:  Popular Library, 1959), and

When the studio definitely decided to proceed with the film,
Karloff was the natural choice for the lead. Although Carlos
Clarens and others have stated that Karloff turned down the part
because he would not be visible until the end of the film,[2] the
truth is that Universal had promised him a pay raise (one richly
deserved after the success of Frankenstein) and then reneged.[3]
Karloff thus refused the role. Whale's second choice for the
part was Colin Clive, but Clive was anxious to return to England
and also declined. This paved the way for one of the most impressive debuts in film history--that of Claude Rains.[5]

---

this has led to claims that Wylie was an uncredited co-author of
the screenplay (John Baxter, Science Fiction in the Cinema (New
York: Paperback Library, 1970), p. 222; Carlos Clarens, An
Illustrated History of the Horror Film (New York: Capricorn Books,
1968), p. 65; Douglas Menville and R. Reginald, Things to Come:
An Illustrated History of the Science Fiction Film (New York:
New York Times Book Co., 1977), p. 46). However, R. C. Sherriff,
the credited screenplay author, told Paul Jensen, "The Invisible
Man," p. 11, that he had never read Wylie's book. After reading
Wylie's heavy-handed, didactic prose, I doubt that he had any
hand in the screenplay. Beyond the general ideas of murder and
invisibility, The Murderer Invisible has no resemblance to The
Invisible Man. As Glut, Classic Movie Monsters, p. 133, suggests,
there may have been vague plans to merge Wells' work with Wylie's,
but The Murderer Invisible seems to have had no direct influence
on Whale's film.

[2]Clarens, An Illustrated History, p. 65. Ron Fry and Pamela
Fourzon, The Saga of Special Effects (Englewood Cliffs, N. J.:
Prentice-Hall, 1977), p. 71, make the same statement.

[3]Glut, Classic Movie Monsters, p. 134; Jensen, "The Invisible
Man," p. 11; and Pendo, pp. 157-158.

[4]Glut, Classic Movie Monsters, p. 134, and Jensen, "The
Invisible Man," p. 11.

[5]Glut, Classic Movie Monsters, p. 134, says that Rains got the
part after Whale saw him in a screen test for RKO's A Bill of
Divorcement. However, Rains stated that the test was the "worst

Before accepting the part, Rains insisted that he be given
star billing, an unheard-of procedure for an actor who had never
appeared in a film, but Universal agreed. This caused the
established Chester Morris to leave the movie, and William Harrigan
was brought in for the part of Kemp. The cast was filled out with
Henry Travers, Gloria Stuart (who had appeared in The Old Dark
House), Una O'Connor (later seen in Bride), Forrester Harvey, E. E.
Clive (who would play the burgomaster in Bride), and a host of
British character actors.

By 1932, the casting had been virtually completed, but there
was no acceptable script. Whale suggested giving his friend, R. C.
Sherriff, a chance; Universal concurred and Sherriff arrived in
Hollywood in April, 1932, while Whale was filming The Old Dark
House.[6]

---

screen test in the history of movie-making" and Whale "howled with
laughter" when he saw it (Jeanne Stein, "Claude Rains," Films in
Review, v. 14 (November 1963), p. 515). Rains was a veteran of the
British stage and Whale had known him in London. This acquaintance and Rains' magnificent speaking voice (a virtual prerequisite
for the part) probably landed the role for him.

[6]Jensen, "The Invisible Man," p. 10, states that Sherriff came
to Hollywood to write a script for The Road Back (later filmed in
1937), was then approached to do The Invisible Man, and actually
wrote the script in England. Jensen bases his information on a
1971 interview with Sherriff, but he quotes events from Sherriff's
autobiography, No Leading Lady: An Autobiography (London: Victor
Gollancz, 1968), which could only have occurred if Sherriff had
worked on The Invisible Man script in Hollywood. This is a con-
fusing area, but I have elected to follow Sherriff's chronology in
his autobiography since he definitely states that he went to Hollywood to write the script for The Invisible Man and it is hardly
likely that his memory would be better in 1971 than in 1968.

The first difficulty which Sherriff encountered was that the
studio had no copy of the original novel! However, they did have
a dozen different tries at adapting the work, and Sherriff had to
wade through them all.[7] He decided that he had to have a copy of
the novel, but he could not locate one anywhere in Hollywood.
Finally, in desperation, he was plundering through a box of old
magazines in the Chinese quarter of Los Angeles when, underneath
the magazines, he came across a tattered, old edition and purchased
it for fifteen cents.[8]

Sherriff modestly asserts that he merely dramatized the novel
on a chapter by chapter basis. However, there are important changes
between the film and the novel. In the film, two characters (Dr.
Cranley and Flora) are added, one (Thomas Marvel) is dropped, and
Kemp's role is changed from a mere acquaintance to an associate of
Griffin's. Sherriff also eliminated the long central portion of
the book in which Griffin describes in detail the events leading
up to his invisibility.

---

[7] Sherriff, pp. 259-260, has amusingly described his problem as
follows: "The man who turned it [the first adaptation] out no
doubt had the original H. G. Wells book beside him, but to justify his
employment, he had got to improve on it. . . . So he had set aside the
original story, and given the invisible man adventures from his own
imagination. The second writer had got to do one better. . . . The
third writer had to trump the one before, and so it went on, each new
effort becoming more extravagant and fantastic and ridiculous. One
writer took the scene to Tsarist Russia at the time of the Revolution
and turned the hero into a kind of invisible Scarlet Pimpernel. Another
made him into a man from Mars who threatened to flood the world with
invisible Martians. . . . One thing stood out clearly in every page I
read. The charm and humour and the fascination that had established
the original Wells story as a classic had been utterly destroyed."

[8] Sherriff, pp. 261-262.

Filming of The Invisible Man did not begin until June, 1933,

and ended in August. This was the longest shooting time for any of

Whale's horror films and was necessitated by the meticulous special

effects sequences created by John P. Fulton (he later won an

Academy Award in 1956 for The Ten Commandments, highlighted by the

"Parting of the Red Sea" sequence).[9] The scenes in which objects

moved by themselves presented no real problems; they were simply

manipulated by thin wires. The scenes with the partially-clad

Invisible Man were the main puzzle. Fulton describes his solution

in the following manner:

> We used a completely black set--walled and floored with
> black velvet, to be as nearly non-reflective as possible.
> Our actor was garbed from head to foot in black velvet
> tights, with black gloves and a black headpiece rather
> like a diver's helmet. Over this he wore whatever
> clothes might be required. This gave us a picture of
> the upsupported clothes on a dead black field.[10]

Fulton then shot the background separately and, by the use of

mattes and an optical printer, combined the shots.[11]

---

[9]The best explanation of how the special effects were created
is by Fulton himself in John P. Fulton, "How We Made The Invisible
Man," American Cinematographer, v. 15 (September 1934), pp. 200-
201, 214. The best general survey of special effects in film is
John Brosnan, Movie Magic: The Story of Special Effects in the
Cinema (New York: St. Martin's Press, 1974). Also of value are
Fry and Fourzon, The Saga of Special Effects, and Rovin, Movie
Special Effects.

[10]Fulton, p. 200.

[11]Briefly, a matte is a covering used to obscure selected
portions of the negative. An optical printer is a machine which
allows two or more different negatives to be combined into one
frame.

This procedure was enormously complicated by the difficulty of directing the stunt man.[12]  He was so tightly wrapped in his black garb (an air hose running up a trouser leg was used to supply air) that he could not hear Fulton's instructions.  Also, in some scenes, it was not possible to leave eyeholes in the helmet and the stunt man had to work blind.  Obviously, this made it extremely difficult to get the actor to move naturally.  As Fulton said, "we had to rehearse and rehearse and make many 'takes'; as a rule, by 'Take 20' of any such scene, we felt ourselves merely well started toward getting our shot."[13]

When the Invisible Man first unwraps his bandages, he pulls off his fake nose and his goggles.  Since it was necessary to show absolute emptiness inside the head, Fulton used a specially constructed, life-sized dummy with a chest designed to simulate breathing.[14]

The sequence in which the Invisible Man's footprints appear in the snow is described below by Ron Fry and Pamela Fourzon.

---

[12]In an interview (see André Sennwald, "That Invisible Actor," New York Times, 3 December 1933, sect. 9, p. 8), Rains implied that he played the stunt parts, but all experts agree (see Brosnan, Movie Magic, p. 72; Fry and Fourzon, p. 70; and Rovin, Movie Special Effects, p. 48) that a stunt man was used. Fulton does not mention Rains in his article.

[13]Fulton, p. 201.

[14]Ibid., p. 200.

Fulton dug a long trench and covered it with a board in which footprint-shaped holes had been cut. The cutouts were replaced, attached to a series of pegs, and the entire construction covered with a layer of plastic snow. A yank on a hidden rope pulled the pegs loose, and the footprints miraculously appeared from nowhere, one by one, as the fake snow collapsed into the holes.[15]

The final scene, where Griffin slowly materializes on the bed, was done by a series of dissolves. Fulton describes it in the following manner:

First, we showed the bed, occupied by its invisible patient: the pillow, indentation and all, was made of plaster, and the blankets and sheets of papier-mâché. A long, slow lap-dissolve revealed the skeleton (a real one, by the way); another lap-dissolve replaced the skeleton with a roughly-sculptured dummy of the actor; and a further series of such dissolves, each time using a slightly more finished dummy, brought us to the real actor himself.[16]

After the final shooting was completed, thousands of frames had to be re-touched by hand to eliminate imperfections picked up by the camera, such as the eyeholes of the stunt man's helmet and the wires used to move objects.[17]

The film was released in November and was well-received critically. Newsweek stated that Wells' novel had been "transferred

---

[15]Fry and Fourzon, p. 71.

[16]Fulton, p. 214.

[17]Fulton, p. 201, said 64,000 frames were re-touched. But, as Jensen, "The Invisible Man," p. 13, points out, this is surely an exaggeration, since 64,000 frames would occupy forty-five minutes of screen time, while the special effects sequences presently take up about fifteen minutes.

to the screen with striking success."[18] William Troy in the Nation
noted that "taken either as a technical exercise or as a sometimes
profoundly moving retelling of the Frankenstein fable, The Invisible
Man is one of the most rewarding of recent films."[19] Mordaunt Hall
of the New York Times said that the film "is in many ways a far
better picture than was Frankenstein" and called Whale's direction
"brilliant."[20] Finally, H. G. Wells himself thought that The
Invisible Man was an "excellent film" and gave Whale the credit for
its success.[21]

## Analysis: The Invisible Man

A mysterious stranger (Claude Rains) enters the Lion's Head
Pub in the small English town of Iping and asks for a room. His
appearance and manners arouse the curiosity of the landlord, Mr.
Hall (Forrester Harvey), his wife (Una O'Connor), and the customers.
The scene shifts to the home of Dr. Cranley (Henry Travers), where
his daughter, Flora (Gloria Stuart), is worried about the disappearance of one of Cranley's associates, Jack Griffin, whom Flora

---

[18]"The Invisible Man," Newsweek, v. 2 (25 November 1933),
p. 33.

[19]William Troy, "The Invisible Man," Nation, v. 137 (13
December 1933), p. 688.

[20]Mordaunt Hall, "An H. G. Wells Story," New York Times,
26 November 1933, sect. 9, p. 5.

[21] H. G. Wells, Experiment in Autobiography (New York:
Macmillan Publishing Co., 1934), p. 475.

loves. Another associate, Dr. Kemp (William Harrigan), tries to force his unwanted attentions on Flora, but she rebuffs him. Back in Iping, the stranger works feverishly with the chemical apparatus which he has set up in his room. When Mrs. Hall interrupts him, he shoves her out the door and throws Mr. Hall down the stairs. A police constable, Jaffers (E. E. Clive), and a group of the townspeople confront the stranger and watch amazed as he unwraps his bandaged head to reveal--nothing! The Invisible Man then escapes. At Cranley's laboratory, he and Kemp search Griffin's room for a clue to his disappearance. They find a piece of paper with the name of a drug, monocane, written on it. Cranley tells Kemp that monocane draws the color from objects, but also induces madness. That night, the Invisible Man enters Kemp's house, identifies himself as the missing Griffin, and explains that he has decided to enlist Kemp (involuntarily) in his plan for world domination. Griffin forces Kemp to take him back to Iping in order to retrieve some books. A police enquiry is underway at the pub; Griffin disrupts it, and kills the Chief of Police (Holmes Herbert). Once back at his home, Kemp phones Cranley and the police. Flora comes to Kemp's and tries to reason with Griffin, but to no avail. The police arrive and Griffin escapes, vowing to kill Kemp. The next night he carries out his threat, and then proceeds to wreck a train and kill numerous members of the search parties looking for him. Taking refuge from a snowstorm in a barn, he falls asleep. A farmer, hearing his breathing, informs the police. They set fire

to the barn, and Griffin is forced to emerge. As his footprints appear in the snow, he is shot and mortally wounded.
Griffin dies in a hospital with Flora by his side, and, as he
dies, his body slowly becomes visible.

The Invisible Man does not contain the somber dignity of
Frankenstein, the symbolic allusiveness of Bride, or the tight,
near-perfect construction of The Old Dark House. Although a
lesser work, The Invisible Man stands as a virtual compendium of
Whale's expertise in stylistic techniques. Furthermore, Whale's
contrast of the ordinary with the fantastic and his union of
farcical humor with scenes of the utmost seriousness make The
Invisible Man an absorbing film.

Whale opens (as he does in Frankenstein, Bride, and The Old
Dark House) on a somber note, with shots of Griffin struggling
through a snowstorm at night toward Iping. He then carefully
establishes the mood of the commonplace with the scene at the
Lion's Head Pub. The rustic villagers are talking, telling jokes,
drinking, and playing darts. The atmosphere is similar to that of
any bar where everyone knows everyone else. Suddenly, with the
entrance of the mysterious stranger, the mood changes. All the
laughing and joking stop; the only sound is the wind howling outside. Griffin's introduction has an obvious stylistic affinity
with the first appearances of the Monster and of the Bride. First,
there is a long shot of Griffin standing in the doorway. Three
villagers are at the right of the frame, the dart board is on the

left, and Griffin is in the center. This is followed by a quick
cut to a low angle medium shot of Griffin, then another quick cut
to a low angle close-up. A muffler covers his chin. He wears dark
goggles and a hat which comes down to the goggles. The rest of
his face is wrapped in bandages.

The appearance of Griffin introduces an element of mystery into
the familiarity of the pub. The warmth and coziness are dissipated,
literally by the storm outside and metaphorically by Griffin's air
of coldness. The upward angle shots, conveying Griffin's haughtiness, are used throughout the film to emphasize his megalomania.
The dark goggles function as an ironic foreshadowing of Griffin's
future. Behind the goggles, he is invisible, but the thick goggles
indicate that he is also blind to his own growing madness. Thus,
while invisible to others, his own madness remains "invisible" to
him. The dark glasses also emphasize Griffin's isolation and
aloneness, a theme stressed repeatedly during the course of the
film.

An excellent example of Whale's mastery of the contrast
between everyday occurrences and the incredible is the scene in
which Griffin describes to Kemp the problems which beset an
invisible man. Griffin and Kemp have just returned from Iping,
where Griffin has murdered the Chief of Police, and he now
lectures Kemp in the following manner:

> Griffin: "There are one or two things you must under-
> stand, Kemp. I must always remain in hiding
> for an hour after meals. The food is visible
> in me until it's digested. I can only work
> on fine, clear days. If I work in the rain,

> the water can be seen on my head and shoulders.
> In the fog, you can see me like a bubble.  In
> smoky cities, the soot settles on me until you
> can see a dark outline.  You must always be
> near at hand to wipe off my feet.  Even dirt
> between my fingernails would give me away.  It
> is difficult at first to walk downstairs, we
> are so accustomed to watching our feet."

During this monologue, Griffin is shown drinking tea, eating toast

and smoking a cigarette.  Whale focuses on Griffin's hands as he

puts sugar cubes in the tea, butters the toast, points the butter

knife at Kemp, and picks up his cigarette.  The scene expertly

blends the most mundane activities (eating, drinking, smoking)

with the totally fantastic.  In addition, its  wit gives Griffin

a human dimension by showing that invisibility has its problems.

The sequence also demonstrates Whale's ability to visually manipu-

late a predominantly verbal scene so that it does not become static.

Thus, there are six shots in the sequence, ranging from a medium

long shot of Griffin and Kemp to a close-up of Griffin's hands, but

all the shots are from different angles and provide a different

emphasis.

An even better example of Whale's combination of visuals with

dialogue is the scene when Flora meets with Griffin.  The primary

importance of this sequence lies in the dialogue; however, Whale,

wisely, has elected not to simply shoot the scene from one position,

but, through camera placement and editing, to supplement the

dialogue with visuals so that a sense of action is maintained.  In

a medium shot, Griffin and Flora are seated by a window with a vase

of flowers in the background. Griffin says, "How beautiful you
look. That funny little hat. I always liked it." In this shot,
Griffin is shown to retain some sense of normality, but the flowers
are an ominous touch. They remain in the center of the frame,
between Flora and Griffin, literally dividing them. Throughout the
sequence, the flowers appear in the frame, in varying positions,
both in focus and out of focus. Their recurring presence indicates
that for Griffin, as for Henry Frankenstein, there is no turning
back, no return to a normal way of life.

As the scene progresses, Griffin's megalomania mounts. Flora
asks him, "Why did you do this?" Whale shoots Griffin's answer in
close-up from a slightly upward angle to show the beginning of
Griffin's delusions of grandeur.

> Griffin: "For you, my darling. I wanted to do some-
> thing tremendous, to achieve what men of
> science have dreamt of since the world began,
> to gain wealth and fame and honor, to write
> my name above the greatest scientists of all
> time. I was so pitifully poor. I had nothing
> to offer you, Flora. I was just a poor,
> struggling chemist."

The dialogue stresses Griffin's mixed motives--impressing Flora,
ambition, self-interest--and introduces a note of self-pity.

As Griffin grows more and more excited, his insanity rises.

> Griffin: "I shall come back to you, Flora. There's a
> way back, Flora, and then I shall come to you.
> I shall offer my secret to the world, with all
> its terrible power. The nations of the world
> will bid for it, thousands, millions. The
> nation that wins my secret can sweep the world
> with invisible armies."

Flora's answer shows her total failure to grasp the extent of Griffin's madness. "Jack, I want you to let my father help you. You know how clever he is. Then we'll have those lovely, peaceful days again, out under the trees, after your work in the evening." In the context of Griffin's insanity, Flora's remarks are absurd, and her "lovely, peaceful days" form an ironic counterpoint to Griffin's vision of "invisible armies" sweeping the world.

Flora's comment about her father's "cleverness" inspires the following reply from Griffin: "Your father, clever. Ha ha! He's got the brain of a tapeworm, a maggot, beside mine. Don't you see what it means? Power, power to rule, to make the world grovel at my feet." Griffin's relationship with Dr. Cranley is clearly shown in this speech. Cranley and Griffin are, in a sense, paired characters, although this motif is not developed as fully as in Frankenstein and Bride. Cranley is obviously an older mentor for Griffin, allowing him to experiment on his own, although Griffin is nominally employed by Cranley. When Cranley learns that Griffin is the Invisible Man (and a murderer), he still refuses to tell the police. In two similar scenes, Whale deliberately unites them. As Griffin sits pondering the solution to his invisibility, he puts his hands on the sides of his head; later, when Cranley learns from Kemp that Griffin is the Invisible Man, he hangs up the telephone and rests his head in his hands in the same posture. Griffin's slighting references to Cranley indicate that, from a Freudian viewpoint, his latent hatred of the "father figure" has surfaced.

Whale shoots Griffin's diatribe, the epitome of megalomania,
in a close-up from an extreme low angle to emphasize his total
madness.

> Griffin: "Power, I said. Power to walk into the gold
> vaults of the nations, into the secrets of
> kings, into the Holy of Holies. Power to make
> the multitudes run squealing in terror at the
> touch of my little invisible finger. Even
> the moon is frightened of me, frightened to
> death. The whole world's frightened to death."

Whale ends the sequence with a long shot to stress the distance
between Griffin and Flora, and between Griffin and reality.

In a parallel scene between Kemp and Flora earlier in the
film, Whale uses some of the same techniques. He begins this
scene with a long left to right panning shot which actually goes
from one room (Dr. Cranley's laboratory) to another (the sitting
room) without a cut, thus stressing that it is not physical, but
emotional, barriers which keep Flora and Kemp apart. Whale ends
this sequence with the camera dollying back away from Flora and
Kemp, emphasizing the distance between them. As in the Griffin-
Flora sequence, a vase of flowers occupies the center of the frame.
Although both Griffin and Kemp desire Flora, this is one flower
("Flora") which, for different reasons, neither can possess.

During a very short episode--which shows the police organizing
search parties, the announcement to the public of the Invisible
Man's existence, and the reaction of the populace to that announce-
ment--Whale exhibits his unique sense of cinematic possibilities
in a remarkable montage sequence which involves three types of

transitions: the wipe, the dissolve, and the cut. This twenty-three shot sequence is only ninety seconds in length and could have been handled in a purely routine fashion, but Whale's attention to detail imbues it with a feeling of precision and movement. The sequence opens with a series of wipes. Though seldom used today, the wipe was a common device in the 1930's and 1940's, often employed to convey a sense of motion. In the first two shots, while the Chief Detective's voice gives instructions to his men on the sound track, Whale plays against the wipe movement (left to right) by reversing the motion (motorcycles and policemen travel right to left) within the shots. In the next two shots, Whale balances the previous ones by having the motion within the shots follow the line of the wipe. The next two shots again reverse the wipe movement. The wipe series ends with a shot of Griffin lying serenely in Kemp's bed.

The next set of shots (eight through thirteen) involves, in each instance, a group of people listening to a radio announcement about the Invisible Man's threat. Whale uses the dissolve, a transitional device whose frequent purpose is to link shots of similar content, to join these shots. The interesting point about shots eight through thirteen is the camera movement. Whale begins this succession of shots with a tracking movement (the camera tracks through a crowded ballroom toward a loudspeaker, parting the dancers as if the Invisible Man were moving through the crowd, thus creating a moment of suspense) in shot eight, continues it in

shots nine through eleven, stops the movement in twelve, and
reverses it in thirteen, thereby achieving a balanced rhythmic
symmetry.

In shots fourteen through twenty-two, Whale uses a set of
very quick cuts (the entire shot progression lasts only fifteen
seconds) to communicate a feeling of frenzied motion and panic.
He mathematically combines these nine shots, all of which show
close-ups of bolts or locks being drawn against the Invisible Man,
into three exact patterned groups by the use of camera placement
and camera angles. Thus, in shots fourteen through sixteen, the
camera angle is tilted right, untilted, and tilted left; in shots
seventeen through nineteen, all three shots are from a slight high
right angle; in shots twenty through twenty-two, the shots are
grouped, respectively, as a low left angle close-up, a high right
angle close-up, and an untilted, straight-on close-up. Shot
twenty-three ends the cycle with a medium shot of Griffin sleeping
peacefully. This entire sequence shows Whale's intelligent understanding of cinematic tools, but, of course, technique, in and of
itself, is of little artistic consequence. In this sequence, Whale
uses these cinematic devices to convey plot information, to
demonstrate the terror and havoc which the Invisible Man is capable
of causing, and to comment ironically on the fear and panic of the
populace while the Invisible Man is quietly sleeping.

Although Whale was a brilliant editor, he also understood
that an excess of editing could be unnecessary and distracting. A

good example of this understanding is Mrs. Hall's first encounter
with Griffin.  As Mrs. Hall moves from the extreme left of the
frame to the extreme right and from foreground to background while
she tidies up Griffin's room, Whale pans and dollies with the
camera, but does not cut.  The emphasis in this sequence is on the
enigma of the unknown stranger.  Thus, as Mrs. Hall moves back and
forth across the room (humorously trying to gain information by
making small talk), Griffin remains in the frame.  Once she leaves
the room, the camera swings back to Griffin "as though connected by
a rubber band or a strong magnetic force"[22] and the scene ends as
it began, with Griffin in the center of the frame.

When Mrs. Hall returns with the food which Griffin has
requested, viewer expectations are aroused that some climax is
imminent, but Griffin is still standing at the window staring into
space.  However, when Mrs. Hall reappears a second time with the
mustard, these expectations are fulfilled.  Mrs. Hall's face as she
opens the door suddenly fills with terror.  Whale cuts to Griffin,
whom the audience expects to see partially invisible, but Mrs. Hall's
reaction of horror is due to Griffin's head being wrapped entirely
in bandages.  During this brief eleven-shot sequence, Griffin is
seen six times, each time from a different angle.  This effect
increases audience uneasiness by keeping the spectator from "settling
comfortably on any single view" of Griffin.[23]

---

[22]Jensen, "The Invisible Man," p. 21.

[23]Ibid., p. 19.

A very important element in The Invisible Man is Whale's use
of humor. Frequently, this humor is simply deadpan, verbal wit.
When Jaffers is informed that he must come to the pub quickly
because "the stranger's assaulted Mrs. Hall and tried to kill her
husband," he remains the image of the staid English policeman and
says calmly, "Oh." After his encounter with Griffin, Jaffers
delivers this opinion, "He's invisible, that's what's the matter
with him." The Chief Detective echoes this sentiment when he
warns his men, "We've got a great responsibility. He's mad and
he's invisible." The verbal and visual wit combine nicely in one
scene where Griffin, expecting the police to arrive at any moment,
is removing his clothes. His back is to the camera and, just as
he unzips his pants, he says, "This'll give them a bit of a shock.
Give them something to write home about. Nice bedtime story for
the kids, too, if they want it." When Griffin and Kemp go to
Iping to retrieve Griffin's books, Griffin tells Kemp, "Don't
stare at me, you fool. Look in front of you." He then kicks Kemp
in the seat of the pants.

This kick is one example of the farcical tricks Griffin plays
while invisible. He pushes over a grandfather clock, breaks
drinking glasses, knocks a drink out of a man's hand, steals a
bicycle and rides off on it, strikes a hat from a man's head, hurls
a rock through a window, steals a cash drawer from a bank and
throws the money to passers-by while singing "Pop Goes the

Weasel,"[24] and, clad only in a pair of pants, chases a woman down
a country road while crooning, "Here We Go Gathering Nuts in May."
This type of humor is obviously meant to be harmless; that is, the
audience does not feel that anyone is really going to be hurt.
Thus, when Whale shifts to another tone, the result is surprised
shock.

The sudden shift of mood occurs in the Lion's Head Pub where
the Chief of Police has just concluded his enquiry. He decides
that all the witnesses have had too much to drink and that the
entire episode is a "hoax." As he starts to dip his pen into the
inkwell to sign his report, the inkwell is lifted up and the Chief
is splattered with ink. Instantly, there is mass confusion.
Drinking glasses fly about the room, Mrs. Hall jumps on top of the
table screaming, "He's here, the Invisible Man," people run into
each other trying to get out of the room, and Jaffers stands in the
midst of the mêlée flailing fruitlessly about him with his night-
stick. Once outside, everyone runs in every direction. The spirit
of the entire sequence has been farcical, a kind of Mack Sennett
Keystone Kops scene. Suddenly, Griffin grabs the Chief, chokes
him to the floor, picks up a stool, and smashes him in the face.
From burlesque, the scene passes to an act of deliberate, brutal

---

[24]This scene gives Whale the opportunity for another gibe
at human nature. Although the populace has been warned about the
danger of the Invisible Man, they ignore this warning and scramble
frantically for the money.

murder. This scene foreshadows those in modern films such as the
absurd bank robbery episode in Arthur Penn's Bonnie and Clyde (1968),
which ends with a bank teller being shot squarely between the eyes.
When Kemp asks what happened, Griffin, with macabre humor, replies,
"Had to take a little exercise to keep warm. Killed a stupid
little policeman. Smashed his brains in."

Although neither Frankenstein nor Bride contains such an abrupt
shift from farce to terror, Paul Jensen notes certain structural
similarities between The Invisible Man and Frankenstein.[25]  Both
films share the idea of a zealous scientist disappearing in order
to work alone, leaving behind a lover, an elderly relative and
ex-teacher (in The Invisible Man, Dr. Cranley combines the roles
of Dr. Waldman and Baron Frankenstein), and a friend who is also
romantically interested in the girl. Also, each film begins with
an ominous scene, shifts to a domestic situation where expository
dialogue is provided (detail-wise, Elizabeth receives a short
letter from Henry, while Cranley speaks of a "note" left by Griffin),
then switches back to the initial situation where the action remains
until a climax is reached (the creation of the Monster, the
"unbandaging" of Griffin).

However, there are important basic differences between the
films. In The Invisible Man, there is no division between creator
and Monster; Griffin is both the creator and the creature. In this

---

[25]Jensen, "The Invisible Man," p. 16.

sense, Griffin is more like Henry Jekyll than Henry Frankenstein (the implications of this point will be discussed below). Another significant difference between the two films is the ending. In Frankenstein, there is a tacked-on happy ending (as in Bride and The Old Dark House); in The Invisible Man, not only does Griffin die, but he also kills Kemp, leaving Flora with no prospective husband.

Kemp's murder is a rather unusual happening in the context of the horror film (in the novel, Griffin fails to carry out his threat). Whale dramatically justifies the killing by his character development of Kemp. In the novel, Kemp is the personification of a typical scientist and is developed as an alternative to Griffin, but, in the film, Kemp is shown to be jealous, surly, and cowardly. In his first appearance, he shows his jealousy and surliness in the following exchange with Dr. Cranley:

Cranley: "Griffin had my permission to work on his own experiments on his own time."
Kemp: "And to clear out whenever he liked and stay as long as he liked?"

Kemp immediately compounds his error by trying to woo Flora at the most inopportune moment and, in the process, verbally attacks Griffin. "He cares nothing for you, Flora. He'll never care for anything but test tubes and chemicals. How can he go away like this, without a word?"

Kemp's cowardice is shown from his first meeting with Griffin. Although he has an opportunity to call the police when Griffin is

out of the room, his fear of Griffin prevents it. After the trip
to Iping, Kemp does call Cranley, and then the police. When Cranley
arrives with Flora, she insists on seeing Griffin. Cranley demurs,
fearful for Flora's safety, but Kemp insists, "He won't harm her.
He was a different man when he saw Flora." After Flora goes
upstairs, Kemp tells Cranley, "We must play for time," hoping the
police will arrive. Cranley, unaware that Kemp has informed the
police, asks, "Why for time?" Cranley wants to cure Griffin, but
Kemp only wants Griffin out of the way. In addition, Kemp reveals
to the police that Griffin is the Invisible Man, after Cranley and
Flora decline to do so, and refuses to cooperate in setting a trap
for Griffin. By this time, Kemp is nearly insane with fear himself.
He tells the police, "I tell you he can walk through solid walls.
He'll kill you all and then come to me."

Although Kemp is a coward and an unappealing character, he is
hardly completely evil and his cowardice, given the nature of
Griffin's bizarre threat, is somewhat understandable. Thus, his
murder still comes as a shock, particularly in light of Griffin's
cold-blooded manner. Kemp is driving on a deserted road, congrat-
ulating himself on escaping from Griffin, when Griffin's voice
suddenly says, "This will do nicely, Kemp." Kemp pleads patheti-
cally for his life, "I'll do anything, everything you ask."
Griffin replies:

> You will. That's fine. Just sit where you are. I'll
> get out and take the hand brake off and give you a
> little shove to help you on. You'll run gently down-
> hill and through the railings, then you'll have a big

thrill for one hundred yards or so, 'til you hit a
boulder, then you'll do a somersault and probably
break your arms, then a grand finish up with a broken
neck. Good-bye, Kemp. You always were a dirty little
coward. You're a sneaking little rat, as well.

How Griffin reached such a state of depravity may be determined
by examining Whale's development of his character. Griffin's
degeneration has been underscored throughout by Whale. As the
film progresses, Griffin regresses, becoming continually more
alienated and isolated. Frequently, he begins a speech in a
normal, reasonable tone, then his fury climbs to demented proportions. When Mr. Hall tells him he must vacate his room, Griffin
"begs" and "implores" Hall to relent. But when Hall is implacable,
Griffin flies into a rage and throws him down the stairs. When
Griffin is confronted by Jaffers (a scene analyzed below), he is
at first only annoyed, but his anger soon flares to fever pitch.
His self-centered lunacy is developed further in his first encounter
with Kemp, who asks the same question as Flora, "Why do it,
Griffin?"

> Griffin: "Just a scientific experiment at first. To
> do something no other man in the world had
> done. But there's more to it than that,
> Kemp. . . . Suddenly, I realized the power I
> held, the power to rule, to make the world
> grovel at my feet. (Griffin shakes his fist)
> I must have a partner, Kemp, a visible
> partner to help me in the little things.
> You're my partner, Kemp. (Griffin points his
> finger at Kemp) We'll begin with a reign of
> terror. A few murders here and there. Murders
> of great men, murders of little men, just to
> show we make no distinctions. We might even
> wreck a train or two. (Griffin leans forward
> with outstretched hands) Just these fingers
> round a signalman's throat."

Griffin begins his monologue rationally, but, as he becomes more
agitated, his voice and his mania grow. Whale shoots the last
portion of Griffin's speech from a low angle, the shot used
throughout to accent Griffin's derangement. This type of shot
occurs in Griffin's introduction, in his confrontation with
Jaffers, in his talk with Kemp, in scenes of him ascending and
descending Kemp's staircase, and in his conversation with Flora.
At the end, there is a reversal of this shot pattern. Griffin lies
in the hospital bed and the camera is above him. As his body
slowly materializes, the camera moves up and away,[26] signifying
that Griffin is now a mere mortal, not a creature of superhuman
power.

In addition to Griffin's megalomania, his isolation and
alienation are repeatedly underlined. Kemp says to Flora that
Griffin always worked "behind barred doors and drawn blinds," and
Griffin's first act in his room at the Lion's Head is to close the
curtains and draw the blinds. At Kemp's, he repeats these actions.
As noted above, his dark goggles also mark his separateness. He
tells Kemp that he began his experiments "five years ago in secret"
and worked "all night, every night, until the dawn," and when Flora
comes to speak with him, he states, "I will see Flora alone."

As stated previously, Griffin is both creator and creature.
Like Dr. Jekyll, he ultimately destroys himself by losing self-control

---

[26]Fulton, p. 214, notes that a special track was built for
this one camera movement.

and by deluding himself that he is omnipotent. Under this illusory
spell of unlimited power, Griffin becomes a murderer, and in terms
of sheer numbers, he is much more of a "monster" than Henry
Frankenstein's creation. According to the Chief Detective, Griffin
kills one hundred people in the train wreck and twenty more among
the search parties. Griffin's murders are also more calculatedly
cruel than the Monster's, and his power is more far-reaching.
Indeed, the police seem completely helpless until Griffin, in the
grip of his megalomania, forgets that he is not without weakness.
Although seemingly invulnerable to man, he is still subject to the
laws of Nature, and a snowstorm provides the means for ending his
"reign of terror." Paul Jensen observes that Griffin faces "the
tragic solitude of a man who has managed to go beyond the normal and
is trapped there, isolated, unable to return."[27] But Jensen misses
the point since, by the latter part of the film, Griffin does not
want to return to "normal" or, more precisely, he would like to be
visible or invisible at will in order to increase his domination of
mankind. Only at the very end does Griffin realize that he should
not have challenged Nature's domain, telling Flora, "I meddled in
things that man must leave alone," thereby recognizing that his
impetuous enquiry has led him only into moral and spiritual darkness.
Like Nathaniel Hawthorne's Ethan Brand, Griffin began to be a fiend
from the moment "his moral nature . . . ceased to keep the pace of

---

[27]Jensen, "The Invisible Man," p. 23.

improvement with his intellect."[28]  Griffin, like Dr. Pretorius,

is a portrait of the "scientist-as-alchemist, who is not disinter-

estedly concerned with knowledge for its own sake, but pursues it

as a means of obtaining power."[29]     The character of Griffin

precisely illustrates "the dangers of power without moral control,

the development of the intelligence at the expense of human sympathy."[30]

The most famous episode (one which exemplifies many of the

techniques, themes, and motifs discussed above) in The Invisible Man

is Griffin's "unbandaging" scene, an "unforgettable"[31] sequence

with a "genuine touch of the macabre."[32]  A shot analysis follows:

Setting:  Griffin's room at the Lion's Head Pub in Iping.

Shot No.

  1-8.    Alternating medium shots of Jaffers and his group
        on one hand, and of Griffin on the other.

Comment:  In this first group of shots, Whale conveys an air
        of expectant confrontation by alternating identical
        shots of each opposing force and holding them for
        the same length of time. He is "setting the stage"
        for the dramatic revelation.  During shot 8,
        Griffin rises and the upward angle shot emphasizes

---

[28]Nathaniel Hawthorne, "Ethan Brand" in Selected Tales and Sketches (New York:  Holt, Rinehart, and Winston, 1950), p. 314.

[29]Bernard Berzoni, The Early H. G. Wells:  A Study of the Scientific Romances (Toronto:  University of Toronto Press, 1961), p. 114.

[30]Geoffrey West, H. G. Wells (New York:  W. W. Norton, 1930), p. 109.

[31]Menville and Reginald, p. 47.

[32]Ivan Butler, Horror in the Cinema, 2nd revised edition (New York:  A. S. Barnes, 1970), pp. 154-155.

his superiority over the villagers, his rising
anger (up to this point, he has been more or less
reasonable, at least from his point of view), and
his megalomania.

Cut to:
9.      Medium long shot of Jaffers and his party.  They
        advance into the room.

Cut to:
10.     Medium close shot of Griffin from the chest up.

        Griffin:  "All right, you fools.  You've brought it
                  on yourselves.  Everything would have come
                  right if you'd only let me alone.  You've
                  driven me near madness, with your gaping
                  through the keyholes and your peering
                  through the curtains."

Cut to:
11-13.  Medium shot of Jaffers (11), low angle close-up of
        Griffin (12), and medium shot of Jaffers (13).

        Griffin:  "You're crazy to know who I am, aren't
                  you?  All right, I'll show you."

Cut to:
14.     Close-up of Griffin.  He removes his false nose and
        throws it at Jaffers.

        Griffin:  "There's a

Cut to:
15.     Medium long shot of Jaffers and his group.  They
        stare down at the object on the table in amazement.

        Griffin:  souvenir  for you,

Comment:  In shots 11, 13, and 15, Whale cuts in the middle
          of Griffin's lines to show the group to whom Griffin
          is speaking.  This is a much more effective way of
          emphasizing the two antagonists than if the camera
          were held exclusively on one group or the other.

Cut to:
16.     Close-up of the fake nose on the table.

Cut to:
17.     Close-up of Griffin.  He removes his goggles and
        throws them at the men.

        Griffin:  and one for you."

Cut to:
18.      Medium long shot of Jaffers and the men as the
goggles land among them. They jump back in fright.

Cut to:
19.      Close-up of Griffin. He begins unwrapping the gauze
around his head.

Griffin: "I'll show you who I am and what I am."

Cut to:
20.      Medium long shot from behind Griffin. He laughs and
continues to unwrap the bandages.

Comment:      In this shot, the effect allows the audience to see
Jaffers and his group's amazed reaction by looking
through Griffin's head, an excellent touch of
grotesquerie.

Cut to:
21.      Close-up of Jaffers.

Jaffers: "Look, he's all eaten away."

Cut to:
22.      Medium shot of Griffin. He throws the gauze at the
men.

Griffin: "How do you like that, eh?"

Cut to:
23.      Medium long shot of the men. They get tangled in
the gauze and retreat from the room in disarray.

Cut to:
24.      High angle medium shot of the group fleeing down
the stairs.

Comment:      The downward angle shot underscores the puniness
and ineffectiveness of the men when matched against
Griffin's madness and invisibility.

Cut to:
25.      Medium shot of Griffin. He is laughing maniacally,
and wipes his invisible forehead with both hands.

Comment:      Griffin's insanity and his total isolation are
conveyed by his crazy laugh and by the fact that
he is alone in the room. The return to the usual
straight-on camera position (as opposed to a tilt)
indicates that conditions will return to normal and
Griffin's triumph will be short-lived.

The impressive point about this sequence is Whale's combination of the special effects with the dramatic action. He is not overwhelmed by the effects, nor does he allow them to cramp his style. Instead, he keeps the film moving by integrating the effects with the editing to produce a fluid, smooth-flowing pace. Thus, he uses low camera angles and dialogue to stress Griffin's madness, and shots of Griffin alone to show his estrangement and solitude. He also cuts frequently during the special effects, a considerably more skillful procedure than the traditional one of setting up the camera in one position and recording the scene from that single set-up.

The pattern of a breach of nature, a period of disruption, and a return to "normality" continues in The Invisible Man. As in Bride, the break has actually occurred before the film begins, but this is not evident until Griffin unwraps his bandages. Then, the chaos and killing begin. As in Frankenstein and Bride, the restoration of the natural order is a pessimistic one, since neither of Flora's suitors remains alive[33] and Dr. Cranley, who is alive, has been identified with Griffin. The subtle (if largely undeveloped) implication suggests that Griffin is an exaggerated version

---

[33]As Paul Jensen, "The Invisible Man," p. 16, observes, "it is tempting to think that Whale . . . consciously decided to 'atone' for his earlier capitulation" in allowing Henry to live in Frankenstein. Although this is a position with which I agree, there is no solid evidence to substantiate the point.

of Cranley and has only done what Cranley, supposedly the
epitome of an "orthodox" scientist, would have liked to do.

As in Bride, the human race is hardly held up as a model for
emulation. The villagers remain their usual ignorant selves; the
police seem ineffective; the general public is easily panicked;
Kemp is a weak coward; Flora has no understanding of the extent
of Griffin's madness and, like Elizabeth, is generally ineffectual;
Cranley is at least partially sympathetic to Griffin, despite
realizing that he is a megalomaniacal killer; and Griffin himself
is a raving madman. Given this situation, the world which Griffin
leaves is unlikely to be free of monsters or madmen.

In the last film to be examined, The Old Dark House, there
are no artificial creatures or invisible men, but only the most
frightening of horror film characters, human beings.

# CHAPTER V

THE OLD DARK HOUSE

> Suppose we're cut off, shut up in
> here, in this house.
>
> Horace Femm
>
> This house is safe.  This house
> is built on rock.
>
> Rebecca Femm
>
> Margaret Waverton:  Oh, Philip, this
>                     is a terrible house.
> Philip Waverton:  It isn't very nice,
>                   is it?

## Background:  The Old Dark House

The most important cinematic precursor of The Old Dark House[1]

is Paul Leni's 1927 film, The Cat and the Canary, one of a series

of "old house" thrillers, which also included The Bat, The Gorilla,

and Seven Footprints to Satan.  Carlos Clarens says that The Cat and

the Canary contains a "genuine sense of mystery";[2] Joe Franklin states

that it remains a "striking and fascinating mystery thriller";[3] and

David Robinson observes that it bears "comparison with Murnau's

German horror films."[4]  Having viewed the film recently, I find

---

[1]The Old Dark House will frequently be abbreviated in the text
as House.

[2]Carlos Clarens, An Illustrated History of the Horror Film
(New York:  Capricorn Books, 1968), p. 55.

[3]Joe Franklin, Classics of the Silent Screen (New York:
Citadel Press, 1959), p. 105.

[4]David Robinson, Hollywood in the Twenties (New York:  A. S.
Barnes, 1968), p. 66.  Considering that Murnau made the striking
Nosferatu (1922), this is a truly incredible statement.

this acclaim difficult to understand. Clarens admits that its
comedy has "aged ungracefully"[5] and Franklin concedes that "it
doesn't survive the years without creaking a little."[6] In fact,
the comedy has "aged" _very_ ungracefully and the film "creaks"
considerably. The humor and the seriousness are never properly
integrated and the comedy sequences are timed so poorly that they
totally destroy the mood of horror. However, the film does have
some virtues. The opening scenes are fascinating. A hand moving
across the screen wipes away cobwebs and reveals the credits. The
next scene shows a purely Expressionist castle-like mansion,
followed by a shot of an old man dwarfed by his medicine bottles
(he is dying) and monstrous cats (representing his greedy relatives).
Then follows a stunning tracking shot through a hallway filled with
shadows and billowing curtains, the prototype of a scene in House
when Eva Moore leads Gloria Stuart through a similar hallway.
Unfortunately, The Cat and the Canary does not sustain these
heights.[7] Its primary influence on House (aside from the obvious
plot similarity of people isolated in an old mansion) lies in its

---

[5]Clarens, An Illustrated History, p. 56.

[6]Franklin, p. 105.

[7]The Cat and the Canary is a good example of the need for
sound to adequately convey a mood of horror. The film would be
much more effective if, for instance, the sounds of the storm
could be heard.

atmospheric, moody sets created by Charles D. Hall, later the art
director for all of Whale's horror films.[8]

House was shot in April, 1932, and released in October.[9]
Benn Levy, a London playwright friend of Whale's, was given credit
for the screenplay (based on J. B. Priestley's 1927 novel, Benighted),
but R. C. Sherriff and Whale himself also worked on the script.  Whale
was apparently given a free hand in selecting the cast and he
brilliantly validates Sherriff's statement that "Whale had an instinct
for finding the right people."[10]  House marked the American film
debuts of Raymond Massey, Charles Laughton (in 1928, Whale and
Laughton had appeared together on the London stage in Levy's play,
A Man With Red Hair),[11] Ernest Thesiger, and Eva Moore.  The cast
also included Boris Karloff (in the first role to give him star
billing),[12] Gloria Stuart, Melvyn Douglas, Lillian Bond, Brember

---

[8]Film design is an area which has been largely neglected in
film literature.  The only work of substance is Léon Barsacq,
Caligari's Cabinet and Other Grand Illusions:  A History of Film
Design, edited and revised by Elliott Stein, translated by Michael
Bullock (Boston:  New York Graphic Society, 1976).  See also Mary
Corliss and Carlos Clarens, "Designed for Film:  The Hollywood Art
Director," Film Comment, v. 14 (May-June 1978), pp. 27-58.

[9]Paul Jensen, Boris Karloff and His Films (New York:  A. S.
Barnes, 1974), p. 50.

[10]R. C. Sherriff, No Leading Lady:  An Autobiography (London:
Victor Gollancz, 1968), p. 197.

[11]Charles Higham, Charles Laughton:  An Intimate Biography
(Garden City, N. Y.:  Doubleday, 1976), p. 15.

[12]Denis Gifford, Karloff:  The Man, the Monster, the Movies
(New York:  Curtis Books, 1973), p. 188.

Wills, and John Dudgeon (actually, "John" Dudgeon was Elspeth

Dudgeon, a young woman who plays the part of a 102-year-old man).[13]

The film was not considered an important release, and no major

periodical even bothered to review it. The New York Times said

"this production . . . is chiefly remarkable for the performance

of the players for the tale itself is disappointing and incomplete."[14]

Harrison's Reports, a Hollywood trade paper, noted that "the

individual performances are so excellent that the story is believ-

able,"[15] and Film Weekly, a British film magazine, reported that

House was composed of "as fine a company of players as one could

wish to see in any picture."[16]  Thus, the few reviews praised the

acting, but found nothing else to say about the film. House also

did not fare well financially, probably because audiences were

disappointed with the lack of physical action in the movie and

were disconcerted by the sudden shifts between tension and comedy.

---

[13]Charles Higham, "Introduction," in Passport to Hollywood: Film Immigrants Anthology, eds. Don Whittemore and Philip Alan Cecchettini (New York: McGraw-Hill, 1976), p. 16.

[14]Mordaunt Hall, "The Old Dark House," New York Times, 6 November 1932, sect. 9, p. 5.

[15]Quoted in Richard Bojarski and Kenneth Beale, The Films of Boris Karloff (Secaucus, N. J.: Citadel Press, 1974), p. 78.

[16]Quoted in Gifford, Karloff, p. 188.

However, many present-day critics find House a re-discovered classic,[17] one of the peaks of Whale's career and of the horror film. Michel Laclos calls it "the most totally successful of James Whale's films";[18] William K. Everson believes it is one of Whale's three best films;[19] Roy Edwards states that House is Whale's "finest personal distillation of the bizarre";[20] and Don Whittemore and Philip Cecchettini state that "its brilliant construction rewards repeated viewings."[21] The means that Whale used to achieve this "brilliant construction" will now be investigated.

### Analysis: The Old Dark House

Philip Waverton (Raymond Massey), his wife, Margaret (Gloria Stuart), and their friend, Roger Penderel (Melvyn Douglas), are trapped by a tremendous storm somewhere in Wales and, lost, seek refuge in a strange, old mansion. The house is occupied by a

---

[17]The term, "re-discovered," is literally true. The film was shown theatrically in the early 1950's, vanished, and has only recently resurfaced (in a very limited fashion) in New York during the 1970's (William K. Everson, Classics of the Horror Film (Secaucus, N. J.: Citadel Press, 1974), p. 81).

[18]Michel Laclos, Le Fantastique au Cinéma (Paris: Pauvert, 1958), p. xxii. The French is as follows: ". . . le plus totalement réussi des films de James Whale." The translation in the text is mine.

[19]William K. Everson, "Rediscovery: Journey's End," Films in Review, v. 26 (January 1975), p. 32.

[20]Roy Edwards, "Movie Gothick: A Tribute to James Whale," Sight and Sound, v. 28 (Autumn 1957), p. 97.

[21]Don Whittemore and Philip Alan Cecchettini, "Orientation to James Whale," in Passport to Hollywood, p. 277.

fearsome looking butler, Morgan (Boris Karloff), an eccentric old man, Horace Femm (Ernest Thesiger), and his sister, Rebecca (Eva Moore). Soon, two other lost travelers arrive, Sir William Porterhouse (Charles Laughton) and his mistress, Gladys DuCane (Lillian Bond). During the course of the evening, Morgan gets drunk and attacks Margaret, Roger and Gladys fall in love, and Philip and Margaret encounter the 102-year-old patriarch of the family, Sir Roderick Femm (John Dudgeon), in an upstairs bedroom. Sir Roderick warns them about his insane son, Saul (Brember Wills), who is kept locked away on the top floor of the house. Morgan releases Saul, who then attempts to set the house on fire. During a fight with Roger, Saul is killed. The next morning, the travelers leave the house.

As one might surmise from the short synopsis, the plot of House is not an important element in the film. Instead, the significant points are its mood and atmosphere, its character development, and its tight, well-balanced structure. The film functions on several levels. It is a subtle comedy-thriller (Whale blends these two components expertly), a parody of the English class structure and social system, and, like Edgar Allen Poe's "The Fall of the House of Usher,"[22] an almost philosophical consideration of the stifling effect of the past on the present.

---

[22]Hereafter, "The Fall of the House of Usher" will be abbreviated as "House of Usher."

There is, indeed, a striking resemblance between House and
"House of Usher." In both works, we have the feeling that the
house influences the nature of its inhabitants, that it is somehow
"alive." In addition--like Roderick Usher and his sister, Madeline,
in "House of Usher"--the Femms are the last representatives (there
appear to be no children) of an old, decaying family "stained with
time, used up, crumbling from within, awaiting collapse."[23] Also
as in "House of Usher," an atmosphere of foreboding pervades House.
The film has no music, but the constant sound of wind, rain, and
thunder forms a sinister symphony which captures the "whole vague
tumult of the night,"[24] increases the viewer's uneasiness and
fright, and creates the sense of an "unharnessed, mocking, anarchic"
world.[25] The mood of apprehension is increased by Whale's use of
the house itself. The exterior is seen only once, a brief glimpse
through the wind and rain. This ominous establishing shot is
accompanied by Philip Waverton's humorously understated line, "It
might be wiser to push on." Wisely, Whale never shows a clear view
of the exterior (in the brief look that we do have, the house seems
like a cross between the Bates home in Hitchcock's Psycho and the
Victorian mansion in George Stevens' Giant). This allows the house

---

[23]Vincent Buranelli, Edgar Allan Poe (New York: Twayne
Publishers, 1961), p. 77.

[24]J. B. Priestley, Benighted (London: William Heineman ,
1932), p. 284.

[25]Ibid., p. 344.

to function as a "baleful embodiment of evil"[26] and conveys a
sense of "evil desolation."[27] Like the Usher mansion, the Femm
house symbolizes, in Charles Feidelscn's words, "the end of
rational order,"[28] and, in truth, the house is filled with evil,
irrationality, and madness. In Michel Laclos' expressive phrase,
"madness completely bathes" the house.[29] Robin Wood, writing of
Tobe Hooper's The Texas Chainsaw Massacre, says that "the 'terrible
house' . . . signifies the dead weight of the past, crushing the
life of the younger generation, the future,"[30] a statement which
also aptly describes the situation in House. Whale shoots the
after-dinner conversation sequence in a variety of close, medium,
and long shots with the camera frequently positioned behind the
fire, so that the scene has an eerie, hazy texture, reflecting the
vague, frightening quality of the Femms' minds. The Femms represent the Victorian past, their minds "so clouded over that they
cannot recognize the needs and desires of the postwar generation."[31]
The guests represent the present and the future which is threatened
by that past.

---

[26]Everson, Classics of the Horror Film, p. 83.

[27]Priestley, p. 292.

[28]Charles Feidelson, Symbolism and American Literature (Chicago:
University of Chicago Press, 1953), p. 35.

[29]Laclos, p. xxii. The French reads as follows: "La folie
baigne entièrement. . . ." The translation in the text is mine.

[30]Robin Wood, "Return of the Repressed," Film Comment, v. 14
(July-August 1978), p. 31.

[31]Whittemore and Cecchettini, p. 278.

The film is structured by a series of scenes involving strong contrasts and sudden shifts, and this structure warrants close examination. Thus, Don Whittemore and Philip Cecchettini identify two "poles of attraction,"[32] Morgan and Saul, and Whale deftly swings the focus of attention back and forth between these "poles." The implicit menace in the house seems physically embodied in Morgan. Like the House, Morgan is mute, and our first view of him is unclear, a shot of an eye peering through a half-open door. The door slowly opens to reveal his sinister, scarred countenance. Whale plays upon the audience's knowledge that this is Boris Karloff, the Frankenstein monster,[33] and their expectation that he will be the danger in the household, to obscure the fact that the real menace, Saul, is offscreen. Whale alternately builds up and plays down Saul's threat by shifting attention to Morgan, the visible danger, and then back to Saul. Morgan's intimidating nature is emphasized in his initial appearance and is further stressed when he is shown secretly watching Margaret while she changes clothes, but his threatening nature is quickly undercut by the fact that the Femms are obviously unafraid of him.

---

[32] Ibid., p. 277. Whittemore and Cecchettini do not elaborate on the film's construction.

[33] Karloff looked so different in House that Laemmle felt it was necessary to add a note at the beginning that this was the same actor who had played the Monster.

Just before the dinner sequence, the terrifying scene between Margaret and Rebecca (discussed below) is followed by Penderel's tension-breaking, disarming comment to Margaret when she enters the living room, "Good for you, Mrs. Waverton, you make it seem like a party." At the dinner table, Saul is mentioned for the first time by Horace, who instantly realizes that he has said too much, breaks off in the middle of a sentence and, in consternation, claps his hand to his mouth. The emphasis then shifts back to Morgan who is covertly eyeing Margaret. This disquieting dinner is interrupted by an ominous pounding on the door. But this threat is dispelled by the entrance of Gladys and Porterhouse, who bring an air of jollity into the house. Porterhouse blusters with infectious cheer, while Gladys performs a frivolous soft shoe dance routine in Penderel's borrowed shoes.

The low-key seriousness of the after-dinner conversation is broken by Rebecca's foreboding announcement, made to the accompaniment of crashing thunder, "Morgan's at the bottle again." (Whale simultaneously stresses and parodies Morgan's menace by a peal of thunder each time his name is called.) The conversation breaks up, and Penderel suggests to Gladys that he venture out to the car to retrieve a flask of whiskey. As Gladys waits just outside for Penderel to return, the door mysteriously shuts. Frightened, she runs around the corner of the house and stops by the kitchen window. Morgan, drunk inside, lurches to the window, smashes it, and makes a grab for Gladys. She runs off in terror--straight into Penderel's

arms. The peaceful, romantic--and ironic--interlude in the car
follows. Meanwhile, the lights go out in the house and Philip
goes upstairs to bring down a lamp. Our apprehension is increased
because Horace refuses to accompany Philip; instead, he locks
himself in his room. The tension mounts as the camera, in a subjective shot, prowls the top floor hallway with Philip, revealing
a double bolted door and a tray of food dishes outside. Obviously,
the creature behind this door must be the fearsome Saul Femm. The
suspense is then dissipated slightly by a cut to the dining room,
where Margaret is trying to amuse and calm herself by playing a
"shadow game"; she uses the candlelight to cast shadows of her
hands on the wall. Suddenly, Rebecca's shadow unexpectedly appears
in the frame and Margaret wheels around in fright, but she sees
no one.[34] However, Morgan abruptly enters and promptly assaults
Margaret, transforming her imaginary nightmare into a real one.
To convey Morgan's dangerousness, Whale uses a variation of the
three-shot sequence used to introduce the Monster, the Bride, and
Griffin. There is a full face close-up of Morgan, a quick cut to
an extreme close-up of his eyes and nose, then another quick cut
to an extreme close-up of his mouth. Hearing Margaret's screams,
Philip races to help her, but his blows have no effect. In
desperation, Margaret throws the lamp at Morgan and knocks him
out. The tension is then relaxed by verbal comedy. Margaret sobs

---

[34]Everson, Classics of the Horror Film, p. 82, correctly
notes the resemblance of this scene to similar sequences in Val
Lewton's horror films of the 1940's.

in a shaken voice, "Oh, Philip, this is a terrible house." Un-
flappable, he replies, "It isn't very nice, is it?"

The emphasis switches back to Saul when Margaret and Philip,
hearing a faint noise, investigate and find Sir Roderick in an
upstairs bedroom. He tells them that Morgan is a "savage" but
must be retained because he is the only one capable of controlling
Saul, who "just wants to destroy and kill." The quiet talk with
Sir Roderick is interrupted by the dramatic news that Morgan has
released Saul. The climactic scene follows (analyzed below) and
involves two reversals, as Whale neatly double bluffs his audience.

Whale skillfully uses this alternating contrast-shift pattern
to manipulate audience emotion; the effect is to leave us unsure
how to react to the film (Hitchcock's best films function in the
same manner). In other words, should House be taken humorously
or seriously? In the dénoument, the appearance of the meek-looking,
servile Saul releases the carefully built-up tension about this
"monster" and we feel that all the talk about madness, insanity, and
destruction has been only a joke. But, suddenly, Whale perversely
plays the climax straight and our preconceptions are again upset as
we realize that we are watching a true psychotic, and not a mild-
mannered victim of family persecution.

A secondary structuring pattern (one which allies House with
Frankenstein and Bride) within the primary contrast-shift organi-
zation is vertical movement.       Horace and Rebecca are introduced as they come down the stairs; Philip goes up the stairs to
find Saul's double bolted door, and then must run down to aid

Margaret; Philip and Margaret go _up_ to Sir Roderick's bedroom;
Saul comes _down_ in his chilling introduction; and, finally, Saul
and Penderel move from the dining room _up_ to the first floor landing
and then crash _down_ during their climactic fight. This up-down
movement parallels the anxiety-comedy dichotomy. Downstairs,
the Femms appear as a bizarre collection of eccentrics--odd and
amusing, yet harmless. But upstairs lies hidden the family
"skeleton in the closet"--the total madness of Saul. Thus, the
outward image of eccentricity masks the inner reality of insanity.

_House_'s composition is theatrical, using a group of "scenes"
in which only two or three people are "on stage." Hence, there
are scenes involving Margaret and Rebecca; Morgan and Margaret;
Horace and Penderel; Horace and Philip; Gladys and Penderel;
Sir Roderick, Margaret, and Philip; and Saul and Penderel. However, as William Everson points out, if the method is theatrical,
the execution remains purely cinematic.[35] This cinematic execution
is evidenced by Whale's initial presentation of each character;
the character's introduction gives us hints of that person's basic
nature. In the first scene, we see the Wavertons in the
front seat of their car bickering sharply, indicating their
"wavering" marriage. As the camera pulls back, we are confronted
with Roger Penderel in the back seat. He is lounging in a
cavalier, insouciant manner, with his feet propped up and a cigarette dangling from his hand, his entire attitude reflected in

---

[35]Everson, _Classics of the Horror Film_ p. 81.

his posture. Sir William Porterhouse and Gladys DuCane burst out
of the night straight toward the camera, bringing an air of vi-
tality with them. Gladys is flighty and flippant; Porterhouse
is bluff and hearty. Horace Femm marches downs the stairs, his
nose uptilted. The camera tracks up toward him as he moves down,
the lighting and camera movement accenting his thin body and his
air of haughtiness and coldness. Rebecca Femm bustles down the
stairs, a fat, waddling old woman. Her initial comments, "What do
they want?" and "No beds, they can't have beds," demonstrate her
sour personality. Sir Roderick is first glimpsed unclearly from a
distance. The long shot emphasizes his "unclear" mind, hazed over
by time and illness. Morgan's introduction, noted above, establishes
his menacing quality immediately. The most effective introduction,
Saul's, will be discussed below.

For such a short film (it runs barely seventy minutes),
Whale is able to portray his ten characters and their relationships with surprising depth. The disintegrating marriage of the
Wavertons (the blandest, least interesting characters in the film)
appears to gain strength from the night's events. After arguing
in the car, Margaret returns from changing her clothes and tells
Philip, "You must have thought I was a long time." He answers
curtly, "Matter of fact, I thought you were quicker than usual."
However, after they have cooperated in knocking out Morgan, he
tenderly says to her, "Take my hand, darling," and they climb the stairs
into the darkness, their reconciliation apparently having begun.

But, as Whale makes clear during the course of the film, any
accord reached in this house of evil and madness is doomed to
failure.

Sir William Porterhouse seems a solid, substantial man
(much like a "porterhouse" steak), but beneath his cheerful
exterior lies a secret. When challenged to tell what started
him on the road to wealth, he unexpectedly replies, "A cotton
frock." He explains that, as a young man, he and his wife had
gone to a party where the other wives ridiculed his wife's cotton
frock as cheap and inappropriate. His wife died shortly thereafter, and Porterhouse vowed to destroy those who had humiliated
his wife. "Within three years, I'd wrecked that company. Once
you've started making money, it's hard to stop, especially if
you're like me and there isn't much else you're good at." Gladys
tells Penderel, "Bill likes people to think he's gay," but he is
actually a sad, lonely person, still brooding about his wife and
her "cotton frock."

Gladys resembles Porterhouse because she, too, comes from
a poor, poverty-stricken background and is determined to make
good. After Porterhouse has admitted his past, he is embarrassed
and lashes out at Gladys, "Why don't you tell them who you really
are?" Gladys remarks, "My real name's Perkins. These people here
know a chorus girl when they see one. Incidentally, not a very
good one at that. If I were better at my job, I probably
wouldn't be weekending with you. No, I take that back. I

probably would. You're nice enough. We get on, but. . . ."
Like Penderel, Gladys is at loose ends, drifting and directionless.

Roger Penderel is amusing but cynical, bright but bitter.
His life is aimless and purposeless, "pending" as his name
indicates. In a revealing sequence, Horace offers a toast
to Penderel, "Mr. Penderel, I'll give you a toast that you will
not appreciate, being young. I give you illusion." Penderel
replies, "Illusion! I'm precisely the right age for that."
Horace correctly identifies Penderel as one of those "slightly
battered by the war," and Penderel answers, "Correct, Mr. Femm.
War generation, slightly soiled. A study in the bittersweet,
the man with the twisted smile, and this, Mr. Femm, is very good
gin." Later, Gladys perceptively observes that Penderel "doesn't
fit into these times," and Penderel says, "I don't think enough
things are worthwhile." But, in Gladys, he seems to find something worthwhile. For part of the night, they sit in the car
drinking and talking, and finally agree to try to "make a go of
it" together.

In the novel, Gladys and Penderel's relationship is concluded
tragically when Penderel dies in the fight with Saul. In the
film, Penderel lives, although there are definite indications
that this may be an altered ending as was the case with
Frankenstein and Bride. However, unlike the latter two films,
no concrete evidence exists that the ending was changed,[36]

---

[36]I wrote to the only known surviving cast member, Gloria
Stuart, in an attempt to obtain information on the ending, but
did not receive a reply.

but the movement of the film certainly leads toward Penderel's
death.  In addition, Whale treats the Gladys-Penderel romance
in an ironic, non-serious fashion.  Their affair appears forced
and artificial; it happens far too quickly and casually to be
believable.  In effect, Whale "kid(s) the love scenes in his
smirky, inattentive approach" to them.[37]  Even if one accepts
the love affair at face value, however, the movement toward
disaster is clear.  For instance, as Gladys and Penderel declare
their love for one another, dawn breaks and a rooster crows.
This would seem to herald the dawn of a new day for them, but
just as Gladys, sensing impending doom, begs Penderel not to
return to the house ("No, Roger, no.  Don't let's go back there.
Let's stay here."), the rooster crows for the third time.  Whale,
with his fondness for religious symbols, suggests that Penderel's
return to the house betrays the future which he and Gladys might
have had together.  Penderel's amazing recovery from his fall
also strains credibility.  Penderel and Saul lie twisted together,
obviously either dead or seriously injured.  Gladys cradles
Penderel's head in her lap and weeps.  Suddenly, to her astonish-
ment, he opens his eyes, apparently fully recovered.  This sequence
may well be Whale's skillful satire on the conventional Hollywood
"happy ending."  In the last scene of the film, the travelers

---

[37]Harry Ringel, "A Hank of Hair and a Piece of Bone,"
Film Journal, v. 2, no. 4 (1975), p. 15.  Ringel is writing
about Frankenstein and The Invisible Man, but his comment is
more appropriate for House.

depart; the sunlight is glaring, harsh, and obviously artificial,
as if Whale were stressing the artificiality of the ending.

To return to the characterizations, the five guests illustrate,
in social terms, the new post-war generation.

> Philip Waverton and Roger Penderel represent the generation
> of young men marked by the war. Margaret and Gladys
> stand for the new kind of independent woman who emerged
> in the 1920's, partly as a result of the war's upheaval.
> Sir William Porterhouse is the self-made man whose hatred
> of class niceties and privilege has given him the incentive
> to rise out of poverty and ruin his former employers.[38]

Pitted against the guests are the house's inhabitants, representatives of the past, "the unfortunate outcome of class division
[Morgan's muteness ] and family degeneration [the Femms' madness]."[39]
In this scenario, the house itself represents England, although
this remains largely implicit in the film. In the novel, however,
one passage explicitly equates the house and England. "Treated
with anything like decency, this house would have been a joy, a
miracle. Now they stood there holding a candle to a fallen
empire of craftmanship "[40] (my emphasis).

The Femms are certainly a curious lot. In Paul Jensen's
words, Horace Femm "best reveals Whale's combination of humour
with menace and insanity."[41] From his first appearance announcing

---

[38]Whittemore and Cecchettini, p. 278.

[39]Ibid.

[40]Priestley, p. 292.

[41]Jensen, Boris Karloff, p. 53.

to the Wavertons and Penderel, "My name is Femm, Horace Femm,"
his character is consistently developed as emotionless and
cowardly. After acknowledging his guests' introductions ("Charmed,
I'm sure"), he moves to the fireplace and picks up a bouquet
of flowers. He says, "My sister was on the point of arranging these
flowers," and then casually tosses them into the fire. The per-
versity of this action illustrates Horace's callousness and easy
dismissal of others' feelings. His unfeeling personality is
further demonstrated during the after-dinner conversation when
Porterhouse, trying to lift everyone's spirits, observes that
although they are isolated for the night, they have at least made
new friends. Horace promptly restores the air of melancholy
with his withering comment, "How reassuring!" His basic nature
is brilliantly conveyed by a single line, "Have a po-ta-to,"
which he repeats three times during the dinner scene, each time
with a different inflection and connotation. His remark to the
uneasy Margaret shows grudging miserliness at having to share
his meal; his comment to the bluff Porterhouse cuts him off in
the middle of a sentence and is uttered in a voice filled with
contempt and scorn; and his statement to the amused Penderel
carries a tone of distrust and suspicion.[42] At the beginning of
the dinner scene, Horace's insensitivity is exhibited again when
he describes Rebecca's insistence on saying grace as "my sister's

---

[42]This analysis of Horace's line is elaborated from a discussion by Everson, Classics of the Horror Film, p. 83.

strange tribal habit." He asks Rebecca to thank God "not only
for yourself, but for me, and for Roderick, and for Saul--."
He immediately realizes his mistake and claps his hand to his
mouth. This incident, one of many, demonstrates his cowardice,
which is established early in the film. During the opening conversation, when Penderel states, "This place may be under water
or even buried," Horace, his face showing fear, drops the vase
he is holding and it shatters on the floor. Shortly thereafter,
for no apparent reason, he again displays his anxiety at possibly
being trapped when he says, "Suppose we're cut off, shut up in
here, in this house." He reacts with terror whenever lamps are
mentioned and, instead of helping Philip find the lamp when the
lights go out, he locks himself in his room.

Whale also uses Horace's character for verbal humor.
When Rebecca screams repeatedly, "No beds, they can't have
beds," Horace remarks acidly, "As my sister hints, there are,
I'm afraid, no beds." As he pours a drink for Penderel, he
comments, "It's only gin, you know, only gin." After a pause,
he adds, "I like gin."[43] When the lights flicker, he notes,
"We make our own electricity here, and we are not very good at it."

The real power in the household rests with Rebecca.[44] When
Horace gives Morgan an order, Morgan always looks at Rebecca

_____

[43]As noted in Chapter III, Thesiger uses almost these exact
words in Bride.

[44]The analogy to the Biblical Rebecca is an ironic one.
The etymology of Rebecca is a "rope with a noose, i.e., a young

before obeying, and even Horace recognizes Rebecca's position.
When Porterhouse asks who the owner is, Horace answers, "My
sister is the owner, Miss Femm." Although Rebecca matches Horace's
rudeness and inhospitality with her constant reiteration of "no
beds," she is not a coward. Only in the climactic scene does
she show fear when she begs Morgan to "take him [Saul] back."
When Horace expresses his fear of being trapped in the house,
Rebecca says, "This house is safe. This house is built on rock."
In addition to showing Rebecca's courage, this statement also
demonstrates Whale's inverted religious symbolism. Churches are
often said to be built on rock,[45] but, in this case, the "church"
is a perverted cathedral, a house of Satan rather than of God, a
symbol of the "active existence of malignant evil in our world."[46]
The stability of the house contrasts effectively with the physical
and mental fragility of the Femms, and, in this respect, House
differs from "House of Usher." While the Usher home crumbles with
Roderick and Madeline's death, the Femm home remains solid, although
the family is decaying.

---

woman whose beauty ensnares men" (John D. Davis, A Dictionary
of the Bible (Philadelphia: Westminster Press, 1925), p. 646).
Rebecca was discovered by Abraham's servant, Eliezer, while he
was searching for a wife for Isaac. Eliezer noticed Rebecca
because of her hospitality, generosity, and beauty. These qualities
are all notably lacking in Rebecca Femm.

[45]The idea derives, of course, from Christ's description of
Peter as the rock on which He will build His Church.

[46]Lyle H. Kendall, "The Vampire Motif in 'The Fall of the
House of Usher'," College English, v. 24 (March 1963), p. 453.

At the beginning of the dinner scene, Rebecca berates Horace

for his "mocking, blasphemous tongue," a foreshadowing of her basic

characteristic--religious fanaticism. Rebecca lives in a world

ruled by a vengeful, deaf, Old Testament God. Her deity is a

projection of her own personality, for she is wrathful, bitter,

and partially deaf. Her religious fanaticism is marvelously

communicated in a scene that Jensen describes as "cinematically

the most imaginative sequence" in the film.[47] Rebecca guides

Margaret down a long corridor filled with billowing curtains and

menacing shadows (an allusion to the hallway in The Cat and the

Canary) into a bedroom so that Margaret can change her wet clothes.

As Margaret is changing, Rebecca sits on the bed talking.

> My sister, Rachel,[48] had this room once. She died when
> she was twenty-one. She was a wicked one, handsome and
> wild as a hawk. All the young men used to follow her about
> with her red lips and her big eyes and her white neck.
> But that didn't save her. She fell off her horse hunting
> and hurt her spine. On this bed she lay. (Rebecca pounds the
> bed) Many's the time I've sat here listening to her screaming.
> She used to cry out to me to kill her, but I'd tell her to
> turn to the Lord. But she didn't. She was godless to the
> end. They were all godless here. They used to bring their
> women here. Brazen, lolling creatures in silks and satins.
> They filled the house with laughter and sin! Laughter

---

[47] Jensen, Boris Karloff, p. 54.

[48] The analogy between the Biblical Rachel and Rachel Femm
is straightforward. Rachel was the younger sister of Leah,
but was much more beautiful than Leah. Jacob was so in love
with her that he served her father, Laban, an extra seven years
in order to wed her.

and sin![49] And if ever I went down among them, my own
father and brothers, they would tell me to go away and pray.
(She laughs in a high, cackling voice) They wouldn't tell
Rachel to go away and pray. And I prayed. I left them
with their lustful red and white women. My father's still
alive. He's upstairs. He's very old, very old. He's 102.
He's a wicked, blasphemous old man. You're wicked, too.
Young and handsome, silly and wicked. You think of nothing
but your long straight legs and your white body and how to
please your man. You revel in the joys of fleshly love,
don't you? (She gets up, goes to Margaret, and fingers her
dress) That's fine stuff, but it'll rot. That's finer stuff,
still, (She places her hand on Margaret's chest) but it'll
rot, too, in time.

Throughout this long speech, Whale intersperses shots from

various angles of Rebecca's distorted reflection in the mirror,

causing the reflection to "mirror" the disordered emotions of

Rebecca's mind. Margaret shrinks back from Rebecca's touch and

cries, "How dare you!" Rebecca looks at Margaret a moment,

then calmly leaves the room. But before going out the door, she

stops in front of the mirror and pats her hair into place. This

action, coming just after her dogmatic lecture on vanity, demon-

strates the paradoxical feelings of which humans are composed, the

roles and poses which we all use, and typifies how Whale adds

depth to his films by the use of such small touches. Margaret,

feeling stifled, opens a window, and the fury of the storm, as

if to match the fury of Rebecca's words, rushes in and blows every-

thing off the bedside table. Trying desperately to calm herself,

---

[49]Another parallel with "House of Usher" is evidenced here.
The Usher home, too, was once filled with gaiety, with "Spirits
moving musically/To a lute's well-tuned law" (Edgar Allan Poe,
"The Fall of the House of Usher," in Great Tales and Poems of
Edgar Allan Poe (New York: Washington Square Press, 1963), p. 90).

Margaret sits down in front of the mirror, and the following

sequence occurs:

Shot No.

1. Medium close-up of Rebecca's face reflected in the mirror.

   Rebecca: "Silks and satins."

Cut to:
2. Medium close profile shot of Rebecca's reflection.

   Rebecca: "Laughter and sin!"

Cut to:
3. Medium close profile shot of Rebecca's reflection from a
   different angle than shot 2.

   Rebecca: "Lustful red and white women."

Cut to:
4. Close-up of Morgan in doorway, secretly watching Margaret.

   From this shot to the end of the sequence, Rebecca's
   laughter is heard on the soundtrack.

Cut to:
5. Medium close shot of Rebecca's reflection from a different
   angle than shot 1.

Cut to:
6. Medium close profile shot of Rebecca's reflection from a
   different angle than shots 2 or 3.

Cut to:
7. Close-up of Morgan. This shot is slightly closer than
   shot 4.

Cut to:
8. Medium shot of Rebecca pounding the bed. Her face is
   distorted.

Cut to:
9. Close-up of Margaret's reflection. Her face is also
   distorted.

Panicky, Margaret jumps up and rushes from the room. She realizes

that, intertwined with the fanaticism, there is truth in Rebecca's

sermon, and, in essence, the house itself has pointed this out.

Like the Usher home, the Femm house seems to possess a kind of intelligence or "sentience."[50] The sequence perfectly expresses Margaret's hysterical state, emphasizes Rebecca's warped fanaticism, and increases audience tension by the shots of Morgan. This episode is also an excellent example of Whale's ability to transform a passage from another medium into cinematic terms and mold it to his own purposes. The scene is developed from a short, two-sentence passage in Benighted ("After she had put on her dress, she sat down in front of the little, cracked mirror . . . and hastily, shakily tidied her hair. The familiar reflection brought comfort to her ")[51] and is used to achieve a totally opposite effect.[52]

Sir Roderick Femm, the elderly patriarch, is, paradoxically, the sanest member of the family. In the novel, Priestley describes his room as a "last little outpost of sanity."[53] Although age and senility have incapacitated him and rendered his mind unclear, he remains well aware of the madness which his children represent. Like his namesake, Roderick Usher, Sir Roderick recognizes the "silent, yet importunate and terrible influence [of the house] which for centuries had moulded the destinies of his family."[54]

---

[50]See E. Arthur Robinson, "Order and Sentience in 'The Fall of the House of Usher'," PMLA, v. 76 (March 1961), pp. 68-81.

[51]Priestley, p. 229.

[52]This analysis is developed from a suggestion by Jensen, Boris Karloff, p. 55.

[53]Priestley, p. 349.

[54]Poe, p. 92.

He also laughs at himself, something none of the other Femms are
able to do. He tells Margaret and Philip, "Madness came. We're
all touched with it a little, you see, except me. (Pause) At
least, I don't think I am." However, Sir Roderick's basic purpose
is to impart needed plot information. It is he who informs Margaret
and Philip that only Morgan can control Saul, and he gives the
Wavertons (and the audience) the first direct indication of the
nature of Saul's madness--pyromania. "Saul just wants to destroy
and kill. He wanted to make this house a sacrifice." Just as
Sir Roderick warns Philip and Margaret that Morgan might release
Saul, word comes that Morgan has, in fact, freed him.

Morgan functions in the film as a force, a symbol of nature's
power. He seems to gain in strength as the storm grows in inten-
sity,[55] although Whale somewhat diminishes his threatening quality
by the use of crashing thunder whenever Morgan's name is mentioned.
At first, this is a frightening effect, but repetition undercuts
the menace; yet we are never quite sure that Morgan is harmless.
He does attack Margaret, and he certainly conveys frenzied fury
during the fight with the three men. In addition, we are always
aware that we are watching Boris Karloff, the charnel-house
Monster from Frankenstein. However, Morgan does not merely
represent raw power. Just as he physically embodies the danger

---

[55]In the novel, Horace explicitly identifies Morgan with
nature. "Being little better than a brute, he is very close to
Nature, and these upheavals have a bad effect upon him and then
he takes to drink and that makes him worse" (Priestley, p. 262).

of the house, so his physical defect (muteness) is a manifestation
of the Femms' emotional and psychological incompleteness.  At the
end of the film, when Saul has been killed, Morgan, weeping silently,
tenderly picks him up and carries him upstairs.  The storm is
spent and so is Morgan's fury.  In this scene, the dumb, brutish
Morgan shows more real human emotion than the physically whole
people.  He is more his "brother's keeper" than Saul's own siblings.

Saul Femm's delayed entrance, one of the most effective
moments in Whale's cinema, deserves careful attention.  After
learning that Morgan has let Saul out, the entire company, with the
exception of Horace (apparently still cowering in his room),
gathers at the bottom of the stairs.  Morgan enters the picture
and Rebecca implores him to "take him [Saul] back."  Morgan
slowly descends the stairs and suddenly lunges at Margaret.  A
furious fight ensues with Whale cutting quickly from one angle to
another as the men force Morgan into the kitchen.  Leaving Porterhouse
and Philip to deal with Morgan, Penderel runs back into the living
room and herds Margaret and Gladys into another room (in the midst
of this chaos, Whale's humor is still apparent, as Penderel, in
the middle of the mêlée, states, "There's going to be trouble").
Rebecca, murmuring "the sins of the fathers, the sins of the
fathers," retreats into her room, and Penderel races to the foot
of the stairs.  The climactic scene follows:

Shot No.

1.  Close-up of Penderel.  He mops his brow.

Cut to:
2. Medium shot of Saul's hand.

Comment: For several minutes, Saul has been forgotten in the
frenzy and confusion. Now Whale directs our attention
back to him.

Cut to:
3. Close-up of Saul's hand. Slowly, his face emerges from
the darkness into the light. He is a small, apparently
weak man. His face is frightened.

Comment: This is a masterly touch on Whale's part. Saul's
threat has been built up throughout the film to
enormous proportions. We have seen Horace react
with fear whenever Saul's name is mentioned; Rebecca,
who seems to fear no one except her vengeful God, is
terrified when she learns Saul is loose; Sir Roderick
states that Saul wants solely to "destroy and kill,"
and that only the hulking, powerful Morgan can control
him. We naturally expect a monstrous, awesome figure,
forgetting that none of the other Femms are large or
strong. In the book, Saul is merely an abstract embodiment of evil and madness, and has none of the
dialogue found in the film. The single description of
him states that "he was much bigger than Penderel and
seemed to be unusually powerful,"[56] a description which is
completely the opposite of his appearance in the film.
It seems impossible that this small, scared man can
be dangerous. He is very short, extremely thin, and
his eyes are filled with fear.

Cut to:
4. Long shot of Saul as he descends the stairs.

Cut to:
5. Medium shot of Saul.

    Saul: "Please don't touch me."

Cut to:
6. Medium side shot of Saul and Penderel.

    Saul: "I'm not mad."

---

[56]Priestley, p. 338.

Cut to:
   7. Close-up of Saul. He still has a terrified look.

      Saul: "Don't put me back. Don't let them put me back.
            I'm not mad. I swear before Heaven I'm not mad."

Cut to:
   8. Medium side shot of Saul and Penderel, as in shot 6.

      Saul: "It's just that they've locked me up here.
            They're all wicked. They're frightened of me.
            I know something about them."

Cut to:
   9. Medium shot of Saul on his knees groveling in front of
      Penderel.

      Saul: "Years ago, they killed their sister, Rachel.
            But I won't tell. I swear I won't tell. Don't
            put me back. Morgan is the devil. He beats me."

Cut to:
   10. Medium shot of Saul and Penderel. Penderel, convinced
      all is well, turns to go let Gladys and Margaret out.
      Saul grabs him.

      Saul: "Don't leave me."
      Penderel: "Just sit on the stairs. I'll be right back."

Comment: The intense dramatic let-down of Saul's appearance is
        underscored in shots 5-10 by his frightened voice and
        his mild, meek, subservient manner, as he (literally)
        pleads with Penderel on bended knee.

      Penderel moves away from the stairs.

Cut to:
   11. Close-up of Saul. His face contorts into a demented
      grimace. His eyes glint. His stare is one of madness.

Brilliantly, Whale has pulled a double-bluff. The last shot shows

what Saul really is--a raging, cunning maniac--not a pathetic, help-

less captive. He has been masterfully playing a role, but, for a

moment, Whale convinces us of his sanity and truthfulness. Unable

to open the door, Penderel returns to find Saul with a knife.

Abruptly, the storm ceases, as if unable to compete with the madman's

frenzy. Now obviously insane, Saul spells out his program for
destruction. He wants to cleanse and purify by fire. "My flames
are like knives. They're cold, they burn like ice." This
reiteration of the fire motif links the film to Frankenstein and
Bride, and Saul's predilection for fire helps explain the other
Femms' tremendous fear of him; if the house were destroyed, they
would be trapped in a society in which, to put it mildly, they
have no place. Saul also makes clear the Biblical connotations
of his name. "Did you know my name is Saul? And yours is David?
And it came to pass on the morrow that the evil spirit came upon
Saul and he prophesied in the midst of the house and David played
upon the harp and there was a javelin in Saul's hand and Saul cast
the javelin." As he speaks, Saul toys with the knife, just as he
is toying with the terrified Penderel. Suddenly, he throws the
knife, deliberately missing Penderel by inches. He then grabs a
lantern and tries to set fire to the curtains on the landing.
Penderel struggles with him, they crash through the railing and
fall heavily to the floor. It appears that they are both dead,
but, as Gladys cradles his head, Penderel's eyes open. Morgan
enters and gently carries Saul away. The next morning, in bright,
clearly unreal sunlight, the travelers leave.

The recurring pattern of a break in nature, a period of chaos,
and a return to "normalcy" is followed in House, as in Whale's
three other horror films. The violent storm provides the breech of
the natural order, and events move form one terrifying episode to
another, until the climactic, cataclysmic ending. Unfortunately,

however, the ending is not sufficiently cataclysmic. Allowing
Penderel to live blunts the sharp edge of Whale's pessimism and
is more destructive of the film's mood than the false endings of
Frankenstein and Bride, although Whale's ironic handling of the
Gladys-Penderel romance, the satire of Penderel's sudden recovery,
and the artificiality of the very last scene does salvage the
situation somewhat. However, even if the ending is taken "straight,"
the restoration of order is negative. The Femms, their madnesses
intact, remain alive (with the exception of Saul), and so does
Morgan, who is never seen again after he vanishes up the stairs.
Most significantly, the house, battered but unbroken by the storm,
still stands as a personification of madness, evil, and irrationality.

There can be no doubt that Whale considers the occupants of
the house more interesting than the guests, although he stresses
the Femms' insanity. Long after the guests have been forgotten,
one remembers the emotional deadness of Horace, the religious
dogmatism of Rebecca, the pyromania of Saul, and the brute massive-
ness--yet strangely touching tenderness--of Morgan. As Carlos
Clarens notes, in Freaks, "Tod Browning made circus freaks appear
human; in The Old Dark House, Whale perversely inverts this formula."[57]
Despite its weak ending, House remains a remarkable film, with a construction that artfully blends anxiety and comedy, building audience
tension and releasing it in a faultless balance. It is a film destined to survive the years with little loss of effectiveness.

---

[57]Clarens, An Illustrated History, p. 65.

## CHAPTER VI
## CONCLUSION

What I'm trying to achieve is to
make you see.

D. W. Griffith

The cinema is the truth twenty-four
times a second.

Jean-Luc Godard

The cinema has no boundary.  It
is a ribbon of dream.

Orson Welles

. . . much of Madness, and more of Sin,
and Horror the soul of the plot.

Edgar Allan Poe, "The
Conqueror Worm"

I take all of Whale seriously.

Harry Ringel

### Recurring Patterns in Whale's Films

Although James Whale has not yet received his proper critical

acclaim, today it is obvious that his horror films are quite modern

in concept and execution.[1]  The subject of this dissertation may

thus be highlighted by summarizing his key themes, motifs, and sty-

listic properties.

----

[1]Without doubt, the main problem in dealing with Whale is
accessibility to his films.  An Academy of Motion Picture Arts
and Sciences publication ("James Whale:  A Research Guide," Academy
of Motion Picture Arts and Sciences pamphlet, 1976) states that
both Paul Jensen and Tom Milne are working on book-length studies
of Whale, but neither work has yet appeared.  Apparently, neither
Milne nor Jensen has been able to locate or to study all of Whale's films.

At the core of Whale's work is his concern for morality.
For example, although Dr. Pretorius, Jack Griffin, and Henry
Frankenstein differ in some respects--in Bride, Pretorius is
insane throughout; in The Invisible Man, Griffin gradually becomes mad; in Frankenstein and Bride, Henry is sane, but a
vacillating weakling--they are all alike in their basic dis-
regard for morality.

Dr. Pretorius is the most immoral (or, perhaps, amoral)
character in Whale's cinema. A would-be dictator, he wishes to
rule all mankind by breeding and controlling a race of monsters,
and uses, without moral compunction, any method which will further
this aim. He kidnaps Elizabeth, drugs the Monster when he is of
no further use, and casually dispatches Karl to kill a young woman
in order to obtain the needed young, female heart. He misuses his
scientific knowledge to bolster his insane ambition. Paradoxically,
his program for the creation of life would lead only to death for
millions, for he would use his race of monsters to destroy anyone
who did not agree with his Nazi-like "New Order"; Whale makes
this clear by closely linking Pretorius with death (Elizabeth calls
him a "figure like Death," his laboratory is filled with skeletons
and skulls, he keeps his homunculi in a coffin-shaped box, he
dines on a casket with a skull as a table ornament). Appropriately,
the Monster, when he destroys the laboratory, tells Pretorius he
"belongs dead."

Jack Griffin, of course, illustrates the dangers of "power without _moral_ control "[2] (my emphasis). He moves from conscience-less indifference (he attacks the Halls and the villagers only because they bother him) to acts of irrational and malevolent hatred (the murders of the Chief of Police and Kemp). In the process, he isolates himself totally, forgetting Dr. Cranley and Flora, just as Henry neglects his father and Elizabeth. But Griffin, in his ultimate madness, is psychologically closer to Pretorius than he is to Henry. Like Pretorius, he uses his vast scientific abilities exclusively for evil, to obtain power and domination. Finally, his perverted megalomania ruins him; in the grasp of his delusion of omnipotence, he believes himself invulnerable even to Nature. In essence, Griffin, like Henry Jekyll, destroys himself by not exercising proper control over his mind and by not restraining his power. Thus, he is fittingly invisible, for his deformity, unlike the Monster's, is not physical but moral.

In Henry Frankenstein's case, Whale investigates the inherent ambiguity of ambition and the effect of that ambiguity on a man of weak moral fiber. Henry's disinterested experimentation (Dr. Waldman tells Victor and Elizabeth that Henry's researches "were far in advance of our theories") becomes a desire for personal fame and glory (Henry tells Elizabeth, "I dreamed of being the first to give the world the secret which God is so jealous of-- the formula for life"). The immediate result of Henry's intense ambition is his isolation; he forgets his studies, his father, his

---

[2] Geoffrey West, _H. G. Wells_ (New York: W. W. Norton, 1930), p. 109.

friend, and his fiancée. But the most important consequence of
his aspirations is the creation of the Monster, the very embodiment
of his warped ambition. Henry, however, has not prepared himself
for the "birth" of his creation and, thus, the Monster enters the
world in an untimely fashion. After the creation, Henry's immoral
actions grow; instead of educating and caring for the Monster,
he allows Fritz to torment and torture him. Henry totally abdicates
his responsibilities after the killing of Fritz by turning the
Monster's destiny over to Dr. Waldman. In Bride, he further
demonstrates his lack of responsibility when he comments to Elizabeth
on "what a wonderful vision" the creation of life was, and, despite
his initial protestations, he eagerly aids Pretorius in creating
the Bride. In a sense, Henry deserves more blame than Pretorius,
for, unlike Pretorius, he has a sense of right and wrong; he
knows he is doing wrong, but his weak character prevents him from
acting in the correct (i.e., moral) manner. In addition, Whale's
artful linkage of Henry to his creation shows that, in rejecting
the Monster, Henry is, in effect, repudiating a part of himself,
a part for which he should take a fully aware responsibility.

The Monster is the filmic incarnation of Philip Thomson's
definition of the "grotesque" in literature as "the ambivalently
abnormal."[3] That is, our reaction to the Monster is a conflicting
one; as a creature of death, he incites abhorrence, but when man

---

[3]Philip Thomson, The Grotesque (London: Methuen, 1972),
p. 27. Thomson discusses the concept of the grotesque in literature,
but his definition fits film as well.

denies him sympathy, love, and education, we feel pity and com-
passion for the hapless creature. Like an innocent Adam, he is
trapped in a world he did not make and this world, with its
strong emphasis on outward appearances, rejects him because of
his hideous exterior. Yet inwardly the Monster is very much alive
to human possiblilties. He responds to the hermit's music,
awakens to the love which the hermit extends, and desires that
most basic human need--a "friend." Hence, the Monster is, in
a marvelous paradox, actually more human in feeling and sensibility
than Henry and the "real" humans who torment him.[4]

During the course of Frankenstein and Bride, the Monster
becomes increasingly isolated and increasingly aware of his
isolation. This growing knowledge culminates when he realizes he
"belongs dead." It should be noted that this theme of isolation
recurs in all four films. In The Invisible Man, Griffin becomes
totally alienated as he descends further into madness, and in
House, the Femms are physically isolated from society by their
location, psychologically and emotionally isolated from the present
by the past, and alienated from each other by their individual madnesses.

The Monster's ethical sense is certainly more developed
than man's. As Harold Bloom perceptively observes, Henry's

---

[4]Harold Bloom, discussing the novel, makes the point that the
Monster is more "human" than his creator in "Frankenstein, or the
Modern Prometheus: A Review," Partisan Review, v. 32 (Fall 1965),
p. 613. Many of Bloom's points are also applicable to the film.

"tragedy stems not from his Promethean excess, but from his own moral error" [5] (my emphasis); Henry errs in not accepting responsibility for his creature and thus indirectly perverts the Monster's innocence. By contrast, the Monster makes the right moral decision in choosing to destroy himself, the Bride, and Pretorius.

From Whale's presentation of the Monster as a superior moral being, one may correctly surmise that his estimation of mankind is unfavorable in the extreme. For Whale, humanity corrupts whatever it touches. For example, Whale's religious skepticism is not centered upon Christ's teachings, but upon man's perversion of those teachings. Indeed, the Monster is on two occasions explicitly identified with Christ: in his descent into the crypt, and during his capture by the villagers. The hermit seems a truly good man, capable of redeeming the Monster through the power of love, while the Monster shows himself a worthy candidate for redemption when he atones for his drowning of Maria by rescuing the shepherdess from the lake. But, given the situation, the Monster has no hope of redemption. His peaceful idyll with the hermit is violently interrupted by the outside world, his religious haven (the hermit's hut functions as a religious refuge) is destroyed, and his only friend is dragged away. Henry's attempt to make his creation in mankind's image results in a gruesome parody of man's outward visage. Ironically, had he created a handsome

---

[5] Bloom, p. 614.

creature, society would not have been disturbed and the Monster
would have been accepted, no matter what evil might have been
locked inside him.  Hence, man degrades Christ's message by
judging the Monster solely on his external physical appearance
without regard to his internal spiritual essence.  Significantly,
the Monster destroys a secular religious statue, the symbol of man's
organized religion, rather than the nearby Christ or angel statue, the
symbol  of Christ's true message.  Other than the hermit and the
Monster, the only character explicitly connected in detail to
religion is Rebecca Femm, the espouser of a strict, vengeful, Old
Testament creed, diametrically opposed to the love and kindness
of the hermit's faith.

Science fares no better than religion in Whale's cinema, although he does not oppose science per se.  Rather, he appears to
agree with H. G. Wells' position, as summarized by Norman and
Jeanne Mackenzie:  "Science is only admirable if it is used to
master the brute within man; it is diabolical if it becomes the
servant of the beast within."[6]  But this is largely a theoretical
stand for Whale because he does not present us with a scientific
equivalent of the hermit; i.e., there is no "good" scientist.
Thus, Pretorius is--and Griffin becomes--a power-mad, embryonic
Hitler.  Henry Frankenstein represents a morally irresponsible
weakling, while Kemp shows himself to be a jealous, spiteful
coward.  Dr. Cranley appears to be the image of a respectable

---

[6]Norman Mackenzie and Jeanne Mackenzie, H. G. Wells:  A
Biography (New York:  Simon and Schuster, 1973), p. 126.

scientist, but Whale's artful linkage of him to Griffin shows that he too is a would-be Invisible Man, awaiting only the right moment to display his own madness. Dr. Waldman's superstitious religious scruples prevent him from understanding the Monster ("Only evil can come of it") and, instead of helping Henry accept his responsibilities, he tries to shoulder them for him. For Waldman, this means simply killing the Monster, rather than extending sympathy or instruction to him.

Whale's view of humanity's other members is just as bleak as his view of scientists. Madness taints many of his characters: Pretorius, Griffin, Karl, and Saul are completely insane, while Horace and Rebecca are certainly touched by lunacy. A static past traps others--such as Baron Frankenstein, Porterhouse, and Roderick Femm. Some figures are harmless, but aimless, ineffectual, and no longer masters of their own fatè--such as Victor, Elizabeth, Flora, Gladys, Penderel, and the Wavertons. The physically afflicted characters invariably surpass the "normal" ones is every way. Thus, the Monster and the hermit are morally superior to everyone in Frankenstein and Bride, with the sole exception of the Bride her- self, who, by rejecting the future planned for her, destroys Pretorius' mad dream, while in House, the physically repugnant Morgan shows the purest genuine emotion in the film when he tear- fully carries Saul's body away.

Humanity en masse shows no moral improvement over the main characters. In Frankenstein and Bride, the peasants are easily

transformed into crazed, bloodthirsty mobs, and in The Invisible
Man the populace is ignorant, greedy, and quickly frightened. In
all the films, the "average man" remains stupid, unenlightened, and
basically inhumane.

In addition to this strong thematic continuity, similar
motifs (primarily visual) run throughout the four films. Thus,
the image of fire as creator and destroyer is most fully developed
in Frankenstein, but in Bride too, fire in both its destructive--
the burning of the hermit's hut--and creative--the creation of the
Bride--aspects becomes an important motif. Fire also functions significantly in House (Saul's pyromania) and The Invisible Man (the
police set fire to the barn to drive Griffin out).

Each film opens in darkness, foreshadowing the gloom and terror
to come, and in three of the films (Bride, House, and The Invisible
Man), opening storms convey the turbulent, "stormy" emotions of
the characters, and visualize the chaotic nature of the film's
world. In Frankenstein and Bride, the storm and fire images merge
(in the form of lightning) in the creation scenes.

Hands, a dominant recurring visual motif in Frankenstein
and Bride, emphasize (as does fire) the dual nature--creative
(Henry's hands create the Monster and the Bride) and destructive
(the Monster kills with his hands)--of man; they also define
character (the Monster tries to "speak" with his hands); and
they tie together the two films, which may almost be seen as
one despite their four year chronlogical separation.

Another important motif repeated in each film is the use of
paired characters. The Monster's link to Henry Frankenstein
has been mentioned above. Additionally, both Fritz (in Frankenstein) and Pretorius (in Bride) may be seen as projections of
Henry's baser instincts, the dark side of his nature. In The
Invisible Man, Griffin and Dr. Cranley are joined to show that
Cranley is a potential Invisible Man, and in House the travelers
(representing the present) are paired against the house's inhabitants (representing the past).

Whale's use of flowers and animals also recurs in more than
one film. Flowers are an important visual motif in
Frankenstein, where they initially represent tradition, continuity,
beauty, and happiness; but their function shifts after the Monster's
encounter with Maria, so that they then symbolize ugliness, death,
and sorrow. In The Invisible Man, flowers literally divide Kemp
and Flora, and Griffin and Flora, demonstrating that Flora is a
"flower" which neither man can possess. In Frankenstein, dogs
possess ominous connotations due to their association with death,
darkness, and abnormality. In Bride, an owl represents the
Monster's loss of ignorance and innocence, and lambs strengthen
his religious associations. Just as a cock's crowing indicates
Peter's betrayal of Christ, so a rooster's crowing symbolizes
Penderel's betrayal of his future in House.

Finally both Frankenstein and Bride contain structural
patterns of vertical movement; the pattern is used to emphasize

the height of Henry's aspirations and the depth of his fall.
Vertical movement is a pattern in House too, where the action
moves up and down the staircase to emphasize the distance between
the Femms' outward eccentricity and their inward madness.

Whale's films also exhibit stylistic continuity.[7] The key
to Whale's cinematic style is his use of editing (extended stylistic analyses of most scenes mentioned below may be found in
the appropriate chapters). Although adept at sudden, quick
cuts (the introduction of the Monster, the Bride, and Griffin;
the Monster's capture; the Morgan-Margaret confrontation), Whale's
true genius lies in his more subtle editing--the ability to link
a number of almost unnoticeable cuts so that each shot in a given
scene is slightly varied. This touch is particularly evident in
the creation scene in Frankenstein, the hermit scene in Bride, the
Griffin-Kemp conversations in The Invisible Man, and Saul's entrance
in House.

------------

[7]Continuity is also shown by the fact that Whale worked with
the same actors and technicians frequently. Hence, of his four
horror films, Boris Karloff appeared in three, and Colin Clive,
Gloria Stuart, Ernest Thesiger, Una O'Connor, E. E. Clive, and
Dwight Frye in two. In addition, Jack Pierce handled the make-
up, Charles D. Hall the art direction, and John Fulton the special
effects for all four films. R. C. Sherriff assisted with the
screenplays of two (The Invisible Man, House) and John L.
Balderston worked on two (Frankenstein, Bride). Arthur Edeson
photographed Frankenstein, House, and part of The Invisible Man,
while John D. Mescall operated the camera for part of The Invisible
Man and all of Bride. Clarence Kolster edited Frankenstein and
House, while Ted Kent did The Invisible Man and Bride. Whale
enjoyed working with the same group of people and the overlap of
personnel enabled him to feel at ease, thus creating a comfortable
working atmosphere and contributing to his films' success.

This technique allows Whale to integrate visuals and dialogue so that a dialogue scene does not become static or "stagy." This integration is especially effective in The Invisible Man (examples are the conversations between Griffin and Kemp, Kemp and Flora, and Griffin and Flora, as Whale shoots each scene from a series of varied camera angles) and House (examples include the dinner scene--Whale alternates close-ups of each diner with medium shots of the entire group, and intercuts close-ups of Morgan--and the after-dinner conversation--Whale shoots the scene from behind the fire, giving the sequence a strange, eerie quality).

Whale's editing also includes superb special effects sequences. He is never intimidated by the effects, but smoothly works them into the flow of the film. Examples are the creation scene from Frankenstein, the "unbandaging" scene from The Invisible Man, and, especially, the creation scene from Bride, where the frenzied pace and tilted camera angles stress the irrationality, abnormality, and immorality of Henry and Pretorius' acts.

## Whale's Influence

Whale's films have lost little of their effectiveness over the years because, as noted at the beginning of this chapter, they remain modern in design and production. Thus, the black humor of Bride, in which death is treated in a jocular vein, is carried to its logical conclusion in Stanley Kubrick's Dr. Strange-love (1964), where the prospect of total nuclear annihilation is seen as a joke. Whale's use of sudden shifts and contrasts is

echoed in the early French "New Wave" films by directors like
François Truffaut and Jean-Luc Godard, and in such a key American film of the 1960's as Arthur Penn's Bonnie and Clyde (1968).
But, of course, the most significant influence of Whale's horror
films is found within the horror genre. From Val Lewton's gloomy,
psychological thrillers of the 1940's--such as The Cat People
(1942), The Seventh Victim (1943), and The Body Snatcher (1945)--
through Alfred Hitchcock's claustrophobic, critically acclaimed
films of the late 1950's and early 1960's--like Vertigo (1958),
Psycho (1960), and The Birds (1963)--to the eerie "possession" movies
of the late 1960's and 1970's--such as Roman Polanski's Rosemary's
Baby (1968), William Friedkin's The Exorcist (1974), and Richard
Donner's The Omen (1976)--there is scarcely a single good horror
film which has not felt Whale's influence. I do not, of course,
claim that modern horror films are direct copies of Whale's films,
but that Whale pioneered in the use of themes, motifs, and stylistic
patterns which any modern horror film director must take into
account.

  To suggest the extent of Whale's influence, I have selected
the two films that I consider the most frightening of the past
decade--George Romero's Night of the Living Dead (1968) and Tobe
Hooper's The Texas Chainsaw Massacre (1974).

  Both of these films were made by independent producers outside the Hollywood studio system and were slow to make any critical
impact (the titles in themselves were enough to guarantee rejection

by most critics). The Texas Chainsaw Massacre[8] was made by a group
of University of Texas film students. The story involves five
young people on a day-long outing, who are terrorized by a
depraved, psychotic family.[9]

In Massacre, Hooper presents us with an "unharnessed, mocking,
anarchic"[10] world, similar to the one portrayed in House, a world
in which everything is out of control. The master image of the
film is Leatherface maniacally pursuing his victims with his
whirring chainsaw; but the saw comes to actually control him,
spinning him dizzily around in circles when he tries to stop, in

---

[8]Henceforth, The Texas Chainsaw Massacre will be abbreviated
as Massacre.

[9]The reaction Massacre inspired is typified by the remarks of
Stephen Koch, who called it a "hysterically paced, slapdash, imbecile
concoction of cannibalism, voodoo, astrology, sundry hippie-esque
cults and unrelenting sadistic violence as extreme and hideous as a
complete lack of imagination can make it. . . . The film is quite
badly made . . . barely on the edge of technical competence" (Stephen
Koch, "Fashions in Pornography: Murder as Cinematic Chic," Harper's,
v. 253 (November 1976), p. 110). In fact, the film is more techni-
cally competent than many Hollywood products; as Robin Wood says,
"its mise-en-scène is . . . intelligent . . . inventive . . .cine-
matically educated and sophisticated" (Robin Wood, "Return of the
Repressed," Film Comment, v. 14 (July-August 1978), p. 30), but the
subject matter is undeniably gruesome and people are murdered with
a chainsaw. However, although Mike Simpson says Massacre "leaves
virtually nothing to the imagination" (Mike Simpson, "The Horror
Genre: The Texas Chainsaw Massacre," Filmmakers Newsletter, v. 8
(August 1975), p. 24), there is less actual blood seen on the screen
than in Bonnie and Clyde, The Wild Bunch, Straw Dogs, The Godfather,
and any of Clint Eastwood's "spaghetti" westerns or his "Dirty Harry"
series. As with Psycho, people often think that they see more in
Massacre than is actually shown. Hooper's extremely rapid editing
and judicious camera placement create an illusion of blood and gore
and the spectator's imagination does the rest.

[10]J. B. Priestley, Benighted (London: William Heineman, 1932),
p. 344.

a scene which is simultaneously absurdly comic and terrifying.
Like the other characters, he is out of control, whirling helplessly
in an indifferent, purposeless world.

As noted in the previous chapter, the "terrible house" symbolizes "the dead weight of the past, crushing the life of the
younger generation,"[11] whether that generation refers to the
travelers of House or the vacationers of Massacre. In Massacre,
this relationship of the past to the present is quite specific,
since Franklyn and Sally's parents once owned the defunct slaughter-
house which Leatherface's father and grandfather operated.

As Robin Wood suggests, the real "monster" in Massacre is the
family itself.[12] Madness has touched the family in Massacre just
as it has touched the Femms. Leatherface and his brother are the
ultimate products of family degeneration in the same way that Saul
Femm is. Leatherface's chainsaw is only another version of Saul's
fire. In the Massacre family, women, traditionally a "civilizing,
humanizing influence," are absent (the grandmother is a decaying
corpse), and this "deprives the family of its social sense and
social meaning."[13] Likewise, the only woman in the Femm family is
Rebecca, who is "decaying" mentally and is unable to provide any
type of "civilizing, humanizing influence."

---

[11]Wood, p. 31.

[12]Ibid.

[13]Ibid.

The graveyard humor in Massacre surely owes a debt to House and, more particularly, to Bride. Leatherface's grotesque skidding as he tries to control his chainsaw has been mentioned above, and the father's reaction to Leatherface's destruction of the door ("Look what your brother did to the door") is certainly one of the most understated, comically macabre lines in horror film history, since Leatherface has just finished sawing up four people. Another image of grisly humor is Leatherface, dressed in a coat and tie, sitting down to a cannibalistic family dinner with his brother, father, and grandfather. Finally, the old grandfather, little better than a corpse himself, and his repeated efforts to kill Sally with a hammer (as he used to kill cattle) form a bizarre, surrealistic comic scene.

Night of the Living Dead[14] (arguably the most effective horror film in thirty years, not excluding Psycho) has even more obvious affinities with Whale's canon.[15] The plot of the dead rising to

---

[14]Hereafter, Night of the Living Dead will be abbreviated as Night.

[15]Night was made in black and white by a group of independent Pittsburgh filmmakers on an extremely low budget, $114,000, according to director George Romero (George Romero, "Scaring People to Death on a Shoestring," Writer's Digest, v. 54 (July 1974), p. 26). As with Massacre, the initial critical reaction was negative. Variety shrilly declared that it "casts serious aspersions on the integrity of its makers . . . and the moral health of filmgoers who cheerfully opt for unrelieved sadism" (Quoted in Elliott Stein, "Night of the Living Dead," Sight and Sound, v. 39 (Spring 1970), p. 105), and Roger Ebert, "Just Another Horror Film--Or Is It?" Reader's Digest, v. 94 (June 1969), pp. 127-128, declared the film unsuitable for children (which it probably is).

kill and eat the living plays brilliantly upon our fear of the dead, the existence of an implacable, unexplainable enemy,[16] and the "paranoid fantasy in each of us that the enemy is everywhere and coming to get us."[17]

Significantly, the "night" of the "living dead" is a Sunday night, representing the "failure of religion in a secular age,"[18] and echoing Whale's religious skepticism. The rising of the dead is, of course, a perverse Resurrection, a theme repeatedly stressed in Frankenstein and Bride.

Night uses vertical movement as a structural pattern in the manner of Frankenstein and Bride. At the beginning, Barbara and Johnny drive up the hillside to the cemetery, the living dead comes down toward Johnny, and Barbara escapes down the hill to the farm- house. Once in the house, the film centers on Harry's desire to take refuge in the cellar (down) and Ben's wish that they defend themselves in the main part of the house (up). Ironically, Ben, (the only one of the group remaining alive) is finally forced down

---

[16]R. H. W. Dillard, Horror Films (New York: Monarch Press, 1976), pp. 67, 78, states that there is a rational explanation for the "living dead"; namely, an excess of radiation from a satellite which has fallen to earth. But this explanation is made only in passing by a government spokesman, and the government is shown to be inept and confused. As Charles Derry says, the radiation explanation is a "fuzzy suggestion . . . that quite clearly is not particularly persuasive" (Charles Derry, Dark Dreams: A Psychological History of the Modern Horror Film (New York: A. S. Barnes, 1977), p. 67). For me, one of the film's primary terrors is the inexplicability of the dead's resurrection.

[17]Paul D. Zimmerman, "We Killed 'Em in Pittsburgh," Newsweek, v. 78 (8 November 1971), p. 118.

[18]Dillard, Horror Films, p. 60.

into the cellar and, when he comes <u>up</u>, he is mistaken for one of
the living dead and shot.

Another thematic element which <u>Night</u> shares with <u>Frankenstein</u>
and <u>Bride</u> is its use of hands.  Ben actively uses his hands in
boarding up the doors and windows, he slaps Barbara with his hand
to end her hysteria, and he kills the first living dead to enter
the house by hand (the living dead can be killed by a blow or a
shot to the head, and by burning).  But the positive values of the
hand are offset by shots of the living dead using their hands to
kill and devour their victims, and the film becomes, in Elliott
Stein's graphic words, "a symphony of psychotic hands--the house is
surrounded by endless rows of ghastly, grasping, insatiable hands."[19]

<u>Night</u>'s grisly verbal humor reminds one of Whale's wit.  The
local sherriff, questioned as to how the living dead can be killed,
says, "Beat 'em or burn 'em.  They go up pretty easy."  When asked
to describe the creatures, he states, "They're all messed up, they're
dead."  On discovering the charred bodies of Tom and Judy in the
burned pick-up truck, one of the posse's members remarks "Someone
had a cook-out here."  Perhaps the most memorable line occurs when
the straightfaced government scientist tells a television inter-
viewer the best way to dispatch the living dead:  "Kill the brain
and you kill the ghoul."

The film's pessimism is deep and inexorable.  Romero himself
has described <u>Night</u> in the following manner:  "The film opens with

---

[19]Stein, p. 105.

a situation that has disintegrated to a point of little hope, and
it moves progressively toward absolute despair and ultimate tragedy.
. . . In essence, the ghouls win out."[20]  But Romero does not
extend the nihilism of his own film quite far enough.  As Charles
Derry states, when Ben is killed, "the horror of the living dead
is replaced by another horror:  the inhumanity of the living."[21]
The "inhumanity of the living" is a theme which would have been
very familiar to Whale.

Both Massacre and Night, then, present nihilistic, negative
worlds, in which man becomes, literally, meat to be consumed.[22]
Their bleak endings are what Whale wanted and intended in Frankenstein, Bride and House, but did not achieve due to studio interference.[23]  Dillard's description of Night as a film reflecting "a
life in which moral failure is the natural human condition"[24] (my

---

[20]Romero, p. 26.

[21]Derry, p. 66.

[22]Lew Brighton, "Saturn in Retrograde or the Texas Jump Cut,"
Film Journal, v. 2, no. 4 (1975), p. 25, calls Night and Massacre
"meat movies."

[23]I do not mean to imply that Whale fought vigorously against
the changes.  He apparently did not.  Although his intentions were
different from Laemmle's, Whale was no Erich von Stroheim, but a
studio director who was willing to accept the studio's right to intervene.

[24]Dillard, Horror Films, p. 113.  Curiously, Dillard chooses to
see Night and Frankenstein as opposed films in their ultimate meaning.
He thinks that Henry's actions at the end of Frankenstein indicate
an acceptance of his moral responsibilities.  I feel that if Henry
had chosen to educate and understand the Monster, then, and only
then, would he have fulfilled his responsibility to the creature.

emphasis) is also an excellent description of Whale's films, for as we have seen, moral failure plays a prominent role in Whale's universe.

Whale's characters live in a world of darkness, evil, and madness, personified by the house in The Old Dark House. It stands impervious to the storm, stark testimony to the power of insanity and irrationality. Whether developing the moral deterioration of Henry Frankenstein through two films, or directing a short vignette like the people scrambling frantically for money while the Invisible Man sings "Pop Goes the Weasel," Whale's vision is ironic and forlorn. It is only a few short steps from this extremely pessimistic world to the totally nihilistic modern one exemplified by The Texas Chainsaw Massacre and Night of the Living Dead.

Near the end of his masterly essay on the horror film, "Even a Man Who Is Pure at Heart," R..H. W. Dillard writes, "I hope I have not misled you or disappointed you by promising wonders and offering you only yourself. . . . The horror film is not the sum of art, but it is art."[25] Similarly, I did not intend to promise wonders, but only to offer the despairing and desolate vision of James Whale's horror films as proof of his genius. Each of these four films begins in darkness and ends with a death--a comfortless, death-centered prospect indeed. Yet, as Pauline Kael says, "a work of

---

[25]R. H. W. Dillard, "Even a Man Who Is Pure at Heart: Poetry and Danger in the Horror Film," in Man and the Movies, ed. W. R. Robinson (Baltimore: Pelican Books, 1969), p. 95.

art is a true sign of life"[26] and, in this artistic sense,

James Whale's horror films remain exhilaratingly alive.

_____

[26]Pauline Kael, <u>Going</u> <u>Steady</u> (Boston:  Little, Brown, and
Co., 1968), p. 221.

Journey's End (1930)
Waterloo Bridge (1931)
Frankenstein (1931)
The Impatient Maiden (1932)
The Old Dark House (1932)
The Kiss Before the Mirror (1933)
The Invisible Man (1933)
By Candlelight (1934)
One More River (1934)
The Bride of Frankenstein (1935)
Remember Last Night? (1935)
Show Boat (1936)
The Road Back (1937)
The Great Garrick (1937)
Port of Seven Seas (1938)
Sinners in Paradise (1938)
Wives Under Suspicion (1938)
The Man in the Iron Mask (1939)
Green Hell (1940)
They Dare Not Love (1941)
Hello Out There (1949) - never released

Frankenstein (1931)

Director:  James Whale
Source:    The novel, Frankenstein, by Mary Shelley
Adaptation and Screenplay:  John L. Balderston, Garrett Fort,
           Francis Edward Faragoh
Photographer:  Arthur Edeson
Make-Up:   Jack Pierce
Special Effects:  John P. Fulton
Art Director:  Charles D. Hall
Editor:    Clarence Kolster


Cast of Main Characters:

| | |
|---|---|
| Henry Frankenstein | Colin Clive |
| Fritz | Dwight Frye |
| Elizabeth | Mae Clarke |
| Victor Moritz | John Boles |
| Dr. Waldman | Edward van Sloan |
| The Monster | Boris Karloff |
| Baron Frankenstein | Frederick Kerr |
| Burgomaster | Lionel Belmore |
| Maria | Marilyn Harris |

The Old Dark House (1932)

Director:   James Whale
Source:     The novel, Benighted, by J. B. Priestley
Screenplay: Benn Levy
Photographer:  Arthur Edeson
Make-Up:    Jack Pierce
Special Effects:  John P. Fulton
Art Director:  Charles D. Hall
Editor:     Clarence Kolster


Cast of Main Characters:

| | |
|---|---|
| Margaret Waverton | Gloria Stuart |
| Philip Waverton | Raymond Massey |
| Roger Penderel | Melvyn Douglas |
| Morgan | Boris Karloff |
| Horace Femm | Ernest Thesiger |
| Rebecca Femm | Eva Moore |
| Sir William Porterhouse | Charles Laughton |
| Gladys DuCane | Lillian Bond |
| Sir Roderick Femm | John Dudgeon |
| Saul Femm | Brember Wills |

The Invisible Man (1933)

Director:  James Whale
Source:    The novel, The Invisible Man, by H. G. Wells
Screenplay:  R. C. Sherriff
Photographer:  Arthur Edeson, John D. Mescall
Make-Up:    Jack Pierce
Special Effects:  John P. Fulton
Art Director:  Charles D. Hall
Editor:     Ted Kent


Cast of Main Characters:

| | |
|---|---|
| Jack Griffin/The Invisible Man | Claude Rains |
| Mrs. Hall | Una O'Connor |
| Mr. Hall | Forrester Harvey |
| Flora Cranley | Gloria Stuart |
| Dr. Cranley | Henry Travers |
| Dr. Kemp | William Harrigan |
| Constable Jaffers | E. E. Clive |
| Chief of Police | Holmes Herbert |
| Chief Detective | Dudley Digges |

The Bride of Frankenstein (1935)

Director:  James Whale
Source:    The novel, Frankenstein, by Mary Shelley
Adaptation and Screenplay:  John L. Balderston, William Hurlbut
Photographer:  John D. Mescall
Make-Up:   Jack Pierce
Special Effects:  John P. Fulton
Art Director:  Charles D. Hall
Editor:    Ted Kent
Musical Score:  Franz Waxman


Cast of Main Characters:

Lord Byron                      Gavin Gordon
Percy Shelley                   Douglas Walton
Mary Shelley/The Bride          Elsa Lanchester
Hans                            Reginald Barlow
Hans' Wife                      Mary Gordon
Minnie                          Una O'Connor
The Monster                     Boris Karloff
Henry Frankenstein              Colin Clive
Elizabeth                       Valerie Hobson
Dr. Pretorius                   Ernest Thesiger
Shepherdess                     Ann Darling
Karl                            Dwight Frye
Hermit                          O. P. Heggie

# BIBLIOGRAPHY

Alloway, Lawrence. "Monster Films." In Focus on the Horror Film,
pp. 121-124. Edited by Roy Huss and T. J. Ross. Englewood
Cliffs, N. J.: Prentice-Hall, 1972.

Anderson, Sherwood. "Hands." In Winesburg, Ohio, pp. 27-34. New
York: Viking Press, 1958.

Anobile, Richard James Whale's Frankenstein. New York: Universe
Books, 1974.

Apollodorus. Gods and Heroes of the Greeks: The Library of Apollodorus. Translated by Michael Simpson. Amherst, Mass.:
University of Massachusetts Press, 1976.

Astruc, Alexandre. "La Camera-stylo." In The New Wave, pp. 17-24.
Edited by Peter Graham. New York: Doubleday, 1968.

Aylesworth, Thomas G. Monsters From the Movies. Philadelphia:
J. B. Lippincott, 1972.

Barsacq, Léon. Caligari's Cabinet and Other Grand Illusions: A
History of Film Design. Translated by Michael Bullock.
Revised and edited by Elliott Stein. Boston: New York Graphic
Society, 1976.

Bawden, Liz-Anne, ed. The Oxford Companion to Film. New York:
Oxford University Press, 1976.

Baxter, John. Hollywood in the Thirties. New York: Paperback
Library, 1970.

Baxter, John. Science Fiction in the Cinema. New York: Paperback
Library, 1970.

Baxter, John. Sixty Years of Hollywood. New York: A. S. Barnes,
1973.

Bazin, André. "La Politique des Auteurs." In The New Wave, pp. 137-
155. Edited by Peter Graham. New York: Doubleday, 1968.

Beck, Calvin Thomas. Heroes of the Horrors. New York: Collier
Books, 1975.

Berzoni, Bernard. The Early H. G. Wells: A Study of the Scientific Romances. Toronto: University of Toronto Press, 1961.

Bloom, Harold. "Frankenstein, Or the Modern Prometheus: A Review." Partisan Review, v. 32 (Fall 1965), pp. 611-618.

Bohn, Thomas, and Stromgren, Richard L. Lights and Shadows: A History of Motion Pictures. Port Washington, N. Y.: Alfred Publishing Co., 1975.

Bojarski, Richard, and Beale, Kenneth. The Films of Boris Karloff. Secaucus, N. J.: Citadel Press, 1974.

Braudy, Leo. The World In a Frame: What We See In Films. New York: Anchor Press, 1977.

"The Bride of Frankenstein." Time, v. 25 (29 April 1935), p. 52.

Brighton, Lew. "Saturn in Retrograde or the Texas Jump Cut." Film Journal, v. 2, no. 4 (1975), pp. 24-27.

Brosnan, John. The Horror People. New York: St. Martin's Press, 1976.

Brosnan, John. Movie Magic: The Story of Special Effects in the Cinema. New York: St. Martin's Press, 1974.

Buranelli, Vincent. Edgar Allan Poe. New York: Twayne Publishers, 1961.

Butler, Ivan. Horror in the Cinema. 2nd revised edition. New York: A. S. Barnes, 1970.

Cards of Knowledge. Lausanne, Switzerland: Editions Rencontre, 1976. S.v. "Little Owl."

Chase, Richard. Herman Melville: A Critical Study. New York: Macmillan Publishing Co., 1949.

Church, Richard. Mary Shelley. London: Gerald Howe, 1928.

Clarens, Carlos. "Horror Films." In Rediscovering the American Cinema, p. 42. Edited by Douglas J. Lemza. New York: Pioneer Press, 1977.

Clarens, Carlos. An Illustrated History of the Horror Film. New York: Capricorn Books, 1968.

"Clive of Frankenstein." New York Times, 15 November 1931, sect. 8, p. 6.

Corliss, Mary, and Clarens, Carlos. "Designed for Film: The Hollywood Art Director." Film Comment, v. 14 (May-June 1978), pp. 27-58.

Crisler, B. R. "Port of Seven Seas." New York Times, 15 July 1938, p. 13.

Davis, John D. A Dictionary of the Bible. Philadelphia: Westminster Press, 1925.

Derry,Charles. Dark Dreams: A Psychological History of the Modern Horror Film. New York: A. S. Barnes, 1977.

Dillard, R. H. W. "Even a Man Who Is Pure at Heart: Poetry and Danger in the Horror Film." In Man and the Movies, pp. 60-96. Edited by W. R. Robinson. Baltimore: Pelican Books, 1969.

Dillard, R. H. W. Horror Films. New York: Monarch Press, 1976.

Douglas, Drake. Horror! New York: Collier Books, 1966.

Durgnat, Raymond. Films and Feelings. Cambridge, Mass.: The M. I. T. Press, 1971.

Ebert, Roger. "Just Another Horror Film--Or Is It?" Reader's Digest, v. 94 (June 1969), pp. 127-128.

Edelson, Edward. Great Monsters of the Movies. Garden City, N. Y.: Doubleday, 1973.

Edmonds, I. G. Big U: Universal in the Silent Days. New York: A. S. Barnes, 1977.

Edwards, Roy. "Movie Gothick: A Tribute to James Whale." Sight and Sound, v. 28 (Autumn 1957), pp. 95-98.

Eisner, Lotte. The Haunted Screen: Expressionism and the Influence of Max Reinhardt. Berkeley and Los Angeles: University of California Press, 1973.

Encyclopedia Brittanica, 1969 edition. S.v. "Ikhnaton," by Margaret Stefano Drower.

Evans, Walter. "Monster Movies and Rites of Initiation." Journal of Popular Film, v. 4 (Spring 1975), pp. 124-142.

Evans, Walter. "Monster Movies: A Sexual Theory." Journal of Popular Film, v. 2 (Fall 1973), pp. 353-365.

Everson, William K. American Silent Film. New York: Oxford University Press, 1978.

Everson, William K. Classics of the Horror Film. Secaucus, N. J.: Citadel Press, 1974.

Everson, William K. "A Family Tree of Monsters." Film Culture, v. 1 (January 1955), pp. 24-30.

Everson, William K. "Rediscovery: Journey's End." Films in Review, v. 26 (January 1975), pp. 31-35.

Everson, William K. "Rediscovery: One More River." Films in Review, v. 26 (June-July 1975), pp. 362-366.

Feidelson, Charles. Symbolism and American Literature. Chicago: University of Chicago Press, 1953.

Ferguson, Otis. "Two Films." New Republic, v. 73 (29 May 1935), pp. 75-76.

Fitzgerald, Michael. Universal Pictures: A Panoramic History in Words, Pictures, and Filmographies. New Rochelle, N. Y.: Arlington House, 1977.

Florescu, Radu. In Search of Frankenstein. Boston: New York Graphic Society, 1975.

Florey, Robert. Hollywood d'Hier et d'Aujourd'hui. Paris: Editions Prisma, 1948.

Frank, Alan G. Horror Movies. London: Octopus Books, 1974.

"Frankenstein Finished." New York Times, 11 October 1931, sect. 8, p. 5.

Franklin, Joe. Classics of the Silent Screen. New York: Citadel Press, 1959.

Fry, Ron, and Fourzon, Pamela. The Saga of Special Effects. Englewood Cliffs, N. J.: Prentice-Hall, 1977.

Fulton, A. R. Motion Pictures: The Development of an Art from Silent Films to the Age of TV. Norman, Okla.: University of Oklahoma Press, 1957.

Fulton, John P. "How We Made The Invisible Man." American Cinematographer, v. 15 (September 1934), pp. 200-201, 214.

Geduld, Harry M., and Gottesman, Ronald. An Illustrated Glossary of Film Terms. New York: Holt, Rinehart, and Winston, 1973.

Gifford, Denis. Karloff: The Man, the Monster, the Movies. New York: Curtis Books, 1973.

Gifford, Denis. Movie Monsters. New York: E. P. Dutton, 1969.

Gifford, Denis. A Pictorial History of Horror Movies. London:
Hamlyn Publishing Group, 1973.

Glut, Donald F. Classic Movie Monsters. Metuchen, N. J.: Scarecrow Press, 1978.

Glut, Donald F. The Frankenstein Legend: A Tribute to Mary Shelley
and Boris Karloff. Metuchen, N. J.: Scarecrow Press, 1973.

Gould, Michael. Surrealism and the Cinema. New York: A. S. Barnes,
1976.

Grant, Barry K., ed. Film Genre: Theory and Criticism. Metuchen,
N. J.: Scarecrow Press, 1977.

Greenberg, Harvey . The Movies On your Mind. New York: Saturday
Review Press, 1975.

Hall, Mordaunt. "Frankenstein." New York Times, 5 December 1931,
p. 21.

Hall, Mordaunt. "An H. G. Wells Story." New York Times, 26
November 1933, sect. 9, p. 5.

Hall, Mordaunt. "The Old Dark House." New York Times, 6 November
1932, sect. 9, p. 5.

Hall, Mordaunt. "When Love Is Blind: Waterloo Bridge." New York
Times, 5 September 1930, p. 7.

Halliwell, Leslie. The Filmgoer's Companion. 4th edition. New
York: Hill and Wang, 1974.

Harrington, Curtis. "Ghoulies and Ghosties." In Focus on the
Horror Film, pp. 14-23. Edited by Roy Huss and T. J. Ross.
Englewood Cliffs, N. J.: Prentice-Hall, 1972.

Hawthorne, Nathaniel. "Ethan Brand." In Selected Tales and
Sketches, pp. 300-317. New York: Holt, Rinehart, and Winston,
1950.

Higham, Charles. The Art of the American Film: 1900-1971. Garden
City, N. Y.: Doubleday, 1973.

Higham, Charles. Charles Laughton: An Intimate Biography. Garden
City, N. Y.: Doubleday, 1976.

Higham, Charles. "Introduction." In Passport to Hollywood: Film
Immigrants Anthology, pp. 3-21. Edited by Don Whittemore and
Philip Alan Cecchettini. New York: McGraw-Hill, 1976.

Huaco, George. The Sociology of Film Art. New York: Basic
    Books, 1965.

Huss, Roy. "Almost Eve: The Creation Scene in The Bride of
    Frankenstein." In Focus on the Horror Film, pp. 74-82.
    Edited by Roy Huss and T. J. Ross. Englewood Cliffs, N. J.:
    Prentice-Hall, 1972.

Huss, Roy, and Ross, T. J., eds. Focus on the Horror Film.
    Englewood Cliffs, N. J.: Prentice-Hall, 1972.

Hutchinson, Tom. Horror and Fantasy in the Movies. New York:
    Crescent Books, 1974.

"The Invisible Man." Newsweek, v. 2 (25 November 1933), p. 33.

Jacobs, Lewis. The Rise of the American Film: A Critical History.
    New York: Harcourt, Brace, and Co., 1939; reprint edition,
    N. Y.: Teacher's College Press, 1969.

"James Whale and Frankenstein." New York Times, 20 December 1931,
    sect. 8, p. 4.

"James Whale: A Research Guide." Academy of Motion Picture Arts
    and Sciences pamphlet, 1976.

Jensen, Paul. Boris Karloff and His Films. New York: A. S.
    Barnes, 1974.

Jensen, Paul. "The Invisible Man: A Retrospective." Photon,
    no. 23 (1973), pp. 10-23.

Jensen, Paul. "James Whale." Film Comment, v. 7 (Spring 1971),
    pp. 52-57.

Joyce, James. A Portrait of the Artist as a Young Man. New York:
    Viking Press, 1964.

Kael, Pauline. Going Steady. Boston: Little, Brown, and Co., 1968.

Kaminsky, Stuart. American Film Genres: Approaches to a Critical
    Theory of Popular Film. New York: Dell Publishing Co., 1977.

Kardish, Lawrence. Reel Plastic Magic: A History of Films and
    Filmmaking in America. Boston: Little, Brown, and Co., 1972.

Karloff, Boris. "Memoirs of a Monster." Saturday Evening Post,
    v. 235 (3 November 1962), pp. 77-80.

Kawin, Bruce. "Creative Remembering (And Other Perils of Film
    Study)." Film Quarterly, v. 32 (Fall 1978), pp. 62-65.

Kendall, Lyle H. "The Vampire Motif in 'The Fall of the House of Usher.'" College English, v. 24 (March 1963), pp. 450-453.

Knight, Arthur. The Liveliest Art: A Panoramic History of the Movies. Revised edition. New York: Macmillan Publishing Co., 1978.

Koch, Stephen. "Fashions in Pornography: Murder as Cinematic Chic." Harper's, v. 253 (November 1976), pp. 108-111.

Kracauer, Seigfried. From Caligari to Hitler: A Psychological History of the German Film. Princeton, N. J.: Princeton University Press, 1947; paperback reprint edition, Princeton, N. J.: Princeton University Press, 1970.

Laclos, Michel. Le Fantastique au Cinéma. Paris: Pauvert, 1958.

Lanchester, Elsa. "Letter to the Editor." Life, v. 64 (5 April 1968), p. 21.

Leish, Kenneth W. Cinema. New York: Newsweek Books, 1974.

Lennig, Arthur. The Count: The Life and Films of Bela "Dracula" Lugosi. New York: G. P. Putnam's Sons, 1974.

Lindsay, Cynthia. Dear Boris: The Life of William Henry Pratt, A.K.A. Boris Karloff. New York: Alfred A. Knopf, 1975.

MacKenzie, Norman, and MacKenzie, Jeanne. H. G. Wells: A Biography. New York: Simon and Schuster, 1973.

Manchel, Frank. Terrors of the Screen. Englewood Cliffs, N. J.: Prentice-Hall, 1970.

Manvell, Roger, ed. The International Encyclopedia of Film. New York: Crown Publishers, 1972.

Manvell, Roger, and Fraenkel, Heinrich. The German Cinema. New York: Praeger, 1971.

Marion, Frances. Off With Their Heads! A Serio-Comic Tale of Hollywood. New York: Macmillan Publishing Co., 1972.

Mast, Gerald, and Cohen, Marshall, eds. Film Theory and Criticism: Introductory Readings. New York: Oxford University Press, 1974.

McConnell, Frank. "Rough Beasts Slouching." In Focus on the Horror Film, pp. 24-35. Edited by Roy Huss and T. J. Ross. Englewood Cliffs, N. J.: Prentice-Hall, 1972.

Melville, Herman. Moby Dick. New York: Holt, Rinehart, and Winston, 1948.

Menville, Douglas, and Reginald, R. Things to Come: An Illustrated History of the Science Fiction Film. New York: New York Times Book Co., 1977.

Milne, Tom. "One Man Crazy: James Whale." Sight and Sound, v. 43 (Summer 1973), pp. 166-170.

Monaco, Paul. Cinema and Society: France and Germany During the Twenties. New York: Elsevier Scientific Publishing Co., 1976.

Moss, Robert F. Karloff and Company: The Horror Film. New York: Pyramid Publications, 1973.

Naha, Ed. Horrors: From Screen to Scream. New York: Avon Books, 1975.

Nelson, Lowry, Jr. "Night Thoughts on the Gothic Novel." Yale Review, v. 52 (December 1952), pp. 236-257.

Nichols, Bill, ed. Movies and Methods: An Anthology. Berkeley and Los Angeles: University of California Press, 1976.

Nugent, Frank S. "The Bride of Frankenstein." New York Times, 11 May 1935, p. 21.

"Obituary: James Whale." New York Times, 30 May 1957, p. 23.

"Ogre of the Make-up Box." New York Times, 31 March 1935, sect. 11, p. 3.

O'Hallaren, Bill. "Behind the Scenes at Battlestar Galactica." TV Guide, v. 26 (16 September 1978), pp. 33-41.

"Oh, You Beautiful Monster." New York Times, 29 January 1939, sect. 9, p. 4.

Pendo, Stephen. "Universal's Golden Age of Horror: 1931-1941." Films in Review, v. 26 (March 1975), pp. 155-161.

Plato. "Protagoras." In The Dialogues of Plato, 4th edition, v. 1, pp. 133-191. Translated by B. Jowett. Oxford, Eng.: The Clarendon Press, 1953.

Poe, Edgar Allan. "The Fall of the House of Usher." In Great Tales and Poems of Edgar Allan Poe, pp. 80-101. New York: Washington Square Press, 1963.

"Port of Seven Seas." Time, v. 32 (11 July 1938), p. 42.

Priestley, J. B. Benighted. London: William Heineman, 1932.

Railo, Eino. The Haunted Castle: A Study of the Elements of English Romanticism. London: George Routledge and Sons, 1927.

Ringel, Harry. "A Hank of Hair and a Piece of Bone." Film Journal, v. 2, no. 4 (1975), pp. 14-18.

Robinson, David. Hollywood in the Twenties. New York: A. S. Barnes, 1968.

Robinson, E. Arthur. "Order and Sentience in 'The Fall of the House of Usher.'" PMLA, v. 76 (March 1961), pp. 68-81.

Robinson, W. R., ed. Man and the Movies. Baltimore: Pelican Books, 1969.

Romero, George. "Scaring People to Death On a Shoestring." Writer's Digest, v. 54 (July 1974), pp. 24-26.

Ross, T. J. "Introduction." In Focus on the Horror Film, pp. 1-10. Edited by Roy Huss and T. J. Ross. Englewood Cliffs, N. J.: Prentice-Hall, 1972.

Rotha, Paul. The Film Til Now. Revised edition. London: Hamlyn Publishing Group, 1967.

Rovin, Jeff. From Jules Verne to Star Trek: The Best of Science Fiction Movies and Television. New York: Drake Publishers, 1977.

Rovin, Jeff. Movie Special Effects. New York: A. S. Barnes, 1977.

Sadoul, Georges. Dictionary of Film Makers. Edited and translated· by Peter Morris. Berkeley and Los Angeles: University of California Press, 1972.

Sarris, Andrew. The American Cinema: Directors and Directions, 1929-1968. New York: E. P. Dutton, 1968.

Sarris, Andrew. "Notes on the Auteur Theory in 1962." In Film Theory and Criticism: Introductory Readings, pp. 500-515. Edited by Gerald Mast and Marshall Cohen. New York: Oxford University Press, 1974.

Sennwald, André. "Remember Last Night?" New York Times, 21 November 1935, p. 27.

Sennwald, André. "That Invisible Actor." New York Times, 3 December 1933, sect. 9, p. 8.

Shelley, Mary. Frankenstein, Or the Modern Prometheus. New York: Collier Books, 1961.

Sherriff, R. C. No Leading Lady: An Autobiography. London: Victor Gollancz, 1968.

Simpson, Mike. "The Horror Genre: Texas Chainsaw Massacre." Filmmakers Newsletter, v. 8 (August 1975), pp. 24-28.

Smith, John M., and Cawkwell, Tim, eds. The World Encyclopedia of the Film. New York: World Publishing Co., 1972.

Solomon, Stanley. Beyond Formula: American Film Genres. New York: Harcourt Brace Jovanovich, 1976.

Spark, Muriel. Child of Light: A Reassessment of Mary Wollstone-craft Shelley. Hadleigh, Essex, Eng.: Tower Bridge Publishers, 1951.

"Star Wars: The Year's Best Movie." Time, v. 109 (30 May 1977), pp. 54-62.

Stein, Elliott. "Night of the Living Dead." Sight and Sound, v. 39 (Spring 1970), p. 105.

Stein, Jeanne. "Claude Rains." Films in Review, v. 14 (November 1963), pp. 513-528.

Steinbrunner, Chris, and Goldblatt, Burt. Cinema of the Fantastic. New York: Saturday Review Press, 1972.

Tarratt, Margaret. "Monsters From the Id." In Film Genre: Theory and Criticism, pp. 161-181. Edited by Barry K. Grant. Metuchen, N. J.: Scarecrow Press, 1977.

Thomaier, William, and Fink, Robert. "James Whale." Films in Review, v. 13 (May 1962), pp. 277-289.

Thomas, John. "Gobble, Gobble . . . One of Us." In Focus on the Horror Film, pp. 135-138. Edited by Roy Huss and T. J. Ross. Englewood Cliffs, N. J.: Prentice-Hall, 1972.

Thomson, David. A Biographical Dictionary of Film. New York: William Morrow, 1976.

Thomson, Philip. The Grotesque. London: Methuen, 1972.

Tropp, Martin. Mary Shelley's Monster: The Story of Frankenstein. Boston: Houghton Mifflin, 1976.

Troy, William. "The Invisible Man." Nation, v. 137 (13 December 1933), p. 688.

Truffaut, François. "A Certain Tendency of the French Cinema." In Movies and Methods: An Anthology, pp. 224-238. Edited by Bill Nichols. Berkeley and Los Angeles: University of California Press, 1976.

Tudor, Andrew. Image and Influence: Studies in the Sociology of Film. London: George Allen and Unwin, 1974.

Underwood, Peter. Karloff: The Life of Boris Karloff. New York: Drake Publishers, 1972.

Walling, William. Mary Shelley. New York: Twayne, 1972.

Weinberg, Herman. "Coffee, Brandy, and Cigars." Take One, v. 6 (July 1978), p. 40.

Wells, H.G. Experiment in Autobiography. New York: Macmillan Publishing Co., 1934.

Wells, H.G. The Invisible Man. New York: Pocket Books, 1957.

West, Geoffrey. H.G. Wells. New York: W. W. Norton, 1930.

White, D. L. "The Poetics of Horror: More Than Meets the Eye." In Film Genre: Theory and Criticism, pp. 124-144. Edited by Barry K. Grant. Metuchen, N. J.: Scarecrow Press, 1977.

Whittemore, Don, and Cecchettini, Philip Alan. "Orientation to James Whale." In Passport to Hollywood: Film Immigrants Anthology, pp. 271-278. Edited by Don Whittemore and Philip Alan Cecchettini. New York: McGraw-Hill, 1976.

Whittemore, Don, and Cecchettini, Philip Alan, eds. Passport to Hollywood: Film Immigrants Anthology. New York: McGraw-Hill, 1976.

Wollenberg, H. H. Fifty Years of German Film. London: Falcon Press, 1948; reprint edition, New York: Arno Press, 1972.

Wood, Robin. "Return of the Repressed." Film Comment, v. 14 (July-August 1978), pp. 24-32.

Wylie, Philip. The Murderer Invisible. New York: Holt, Rinehart, and Winston, 1931; paperback reprint edition, New York: Popular Library, 1959.

Zimmerman, Paul D. "We Killed 'Em in Pittsburg." Newsweek, v. 78 (8 Novermber 1971), p. 118.

Zinman, David. Fifty Classic Motion Pictures. New York: Crown Publishers, 1970.

Zoellner, Robert. The Salt-Sea Mastodon: A Reading of Moby Dick. Berkeley and Los Angeles: University of California Press, 1973.

# DISSERTATIONS ON FILM 1980

*An Arno Press Collection*

Allen, Robert C. **Vaudeville and Film 1895-1915: A Study in Media Interaction** (Doctoral Dissertation, The University of Iowa, 1977). 1980

Bordwell, David. **French Impressionist Cinema: Film Culture, Film Theory, and Film Style** (Doctoral Dissertation, The University of Iowa, 1974). 1980

Brown, Kent R. **The Screenwriter as Collaborator: The Career of Stewart Stern** (Doctoral Dissertation, The University of Iowa, 1972). 1980

Cozyris, George Agis. **Christian Metz and the Reality of Film** (Doctoral Dissertation, The University of Southern California, 1979). 1980

Curran, Trisha. **A New Note on the Film: A Theory of Film Criticism Derived from Susanne K. Langer's Philosophy of Art** (Doctoral Dissertation, Ohio State University, 1978). 1980

Daly, David Anthony. **A Comparison of Exhibition and Distribution Patterns in Three Recent Feature Motion Pictures** (Doctoral Dissertation, Southern Illinois University, 1978). 1980

Diakité, Madubuko. **Film, Culture, and the Black Filmmaker: A Study of Functional Relationships and Parallel Developments** (Doctoral Dissertation, Stockholm University, 1978). 1980

Editors of *Look*. **Movie Lot to Beachhead: The Motion Picture Goes to War and Prepares for the Future.** 1945

Ellis, Reed. **A Journey Into Darkness: The Art of James Whale's Horror Films** (Doctoral Dissertation, The University of Florida, 1979). 1980

Fleener-Marzec, Nickieann. **D.W. Griffith's *The Birth of a Nation*: Controversy, Suppression, and the First Amendment as it Applies to Filmic Expression, 1915-1973** (Doctoral Dissertation, The University of Wisconsin, 1977). 1980

Garton, Joseph W. **The Film Acting of John Barrymore** (Doctoral Dissertation, New York University, 1977). 1980

Gehring, Wes D. **Leo McCarey and the Comic Anti-Hero in American Film** (Doctoral Dissertation, The University of Iowa, 1977). 1980

Kindem, Gorham Anders. **Toward a Semiotic Theory of Visual Communication in the Cinema: A Reappraisal of Semiotic Theories from a Cinematic Perspective and a Semiotic Analysis of Color Signs and Communication in the Color Films of Alfred Hitchcock** (Doctoral Dissertation, Northwestern University, 1977). 1980

Manvell, Roger. **Ingmar Bergman: An Appreciation**. 1980

Moore, Barry Walter. **Aesthetic Aspects of Recent Experimental Film** (Doctoral Dissertation, The University of Michigan, 1977). 1980

Nichols, William James. **Newsreel: Documentary Filmmaking on the American Left** (Doctoral Dissertation, The University of California, Los Angeles, 1975). 1980

Rose, Brian Geoffrey. **An Examination of Narrative Structure in Four Films of Frank Capra** (Doctoral Dissertation, The University of Wisconsin, 1976). 1980

Salvaggio, Jerry Lee. **A Theory of Film Language** (Doctoral Dissertation, The University of Michigan, 1978). 1980

Simonet, Thomas Solon. **Regression Analysis of Prior Experiences of Key Production Personnel as Predictors of Revenues from High-Grossing Motion Pictures in American Release** (Doctoral Dissertation, Temple University, 1977). 1980

Siska, William Charles. **Modernism in the Narrative Cinema: The Art Film as a Genre** (Doctoral Dissertation, Northwestern University, 1976). 1980

Stewart, Lucy Ann Liggett. **Ida Lupino as Film Director, 1949-1953: An Auteur Approach** (Doctoral Dissertation, The University of Michigan, 1979). 1980

Strebel, Elizabeth Grottle. **French Social Cinema of the Nineteen Thirties: A Cinematographic Expression of Popular Front Consciousness** (Doctoral Dissertation, Princeton University, 1973). 1980

Veeder, Gerry K. **The Influence of Subliminal Suggestion on the Response to Two Films** (Doctoral Dissertation, Wayne State University, 1975). 1980

Vincent, Richard C. **Financial Characteristics of Selected 'B' Film Productions of Albert J. Cohen, 1951-1957** (Masters Thesis, Temple University, 1977). 1980

Williams, Alan Larson. **Max Ophuls and the Cinema of Desire** (Doctoral Dissertation, The State University of New York, Buffalo, 1977). 1980

INVENTORY 1983